CREATIVITY AND TAOISM

CREATIVITY AND TAOISM

A study of Chinese philosophy, art, & poetry

Chang Chung-yuan, Ph.D.

HARPER TORCHBOOKS
Harper & Row, Publishers
New York, Cambridge, Philadelphia, San Francisco
London, Mexico City, São Paulo, Sydney

*This book was first published in 1963
by The Julian Press, Inc., New York
and is here reprinted by arrangement.*

CREATIVITY AND TAOISM: A STUDY OF CHINESE
PHILOSOPHY, ART, AND POETRY
Copyright © 1963 by Chang Chung-yuan.

First Harper paperback edition published 1970.

ISBN: 0-06-131968-6

89 90   20 19 18 17 16 15 14

Contents

Figures

CREATIVITY AND TAOISM

Introduction

In a witty and profound essay entitled "A Conversation with a Chinese" [1] Voltaire draws a vivid picture of an encounter of a gentleman from China and a Hollander. The meeting occurs in a bookstore where the Chinese has asked for a world history. Skimming through it quickly he discovers to his astonishment that there is not a word in the entire volume about China. Understandably enough he is very upset and falls into discussion about this curious oversight with a Dutch scholar who was present. "How is it possible," he asks when they have become acquainted, "that in a volume entitled *World History* there is not a single word about China?" But soon it is the Hollander's turn to be astonished, for it transpires in their talk that the Chinese visitor had never even so much as heard of Caesar or the ancient Greeks. Voltaire's laconic comment for the entire affair is "Vainglory!"

But less than a hundred years later—in 1816 to be

[1] *The Works of Voltaire,* The Collectors' Edition, Vol. IV, p. 28.

exact—Hegel was lecturing learnedly at Heidelberg on Taoism, Confucianism, and the philosophy found in the *I Ching*. His information, to be sure, was derived secondhand from the translations of the Jesuits, but he was surprisingly well informed, notably on the subject of Taoism. For example, we find in his lectures the following:

> We still have his [Lao Tzu's] principal writings; they are available in Vienna and I have seen them myself. One special passage is frequently quoted from them: "The nameless *Tao* is the beginning of Heaven and Earth; with a name *Tao* is the Mother of the Universe (All Things). . . . To the Chinese what is highest, the origin of things, is nothingness, emptiness, the altogether undetermined, the abstract universal, and this is also called *Tao*. . . ." [2]

In his lecture, Hegel compares Chinese Taoism with Greek thinking:

> When the Greeks say that the absolute is one, or when men in modern times say that it is the highest existence, all determinations are abolished, and by the merely abstract Being nothing has been expressed except this same negation, only in an affirmative form. [3]

From this parallel drawn between Chinese Taoism and Western philosophy it is obvious that Hegel was quite familiar with the philosophy of the East. Thus we see that by the beginning of the nineteenth century Taoism was being carefully examined for its place in the history of philosophy.

About a hundred years later, in 1929, when Richard Wilhelm published his German translation of

---

[2] Hegel's *Lectures on the History of Philosophy*, edited and translated by E. S. Haldane, Vol. I, p. 125.
[3] *Ibid.*, p. 125.

The Secret of the Golden Flower, C. G. Jung wrote an important introduction in which he expounds the essence of *Tao* in the light of modern psychology. He says:

> If we take *Tao* as the method or conscious way by which to unite what is separated, we have probably come quite close to the psychological content of the concept. . . . Without doubt also, the question of making opposites conscious ("conversion") means reunion with the laws of life represented in the unconscious, and the purpose of this reunion is the attainment of conscious life, or, expressed in Chinese terms, the bringing about of *Tao.*[4]

The value of *Tao* lies in its power to reconcile opposites on a higher level of consciousness. It is symbolically expressed as light in Taoism. To reconcile the polarities in order to achieve a balanced way of living and a higher integration is the endeavor of psychotherapy. Jung found out that the method he had applied for years in his practice coincided with the wise teaching of the ancient Taoists. He says:

> My experience in my practice has been such as to reveal to me a quite new and unexpected approach to Eastern wisdom. But it must be well understood that I did not have a starting point, a more or less adequate knowledge of Chinese philosophy. . . . It is only later that my professional experiences have shown me that in my technique I had been unconsciously led along the secret way which for centuries has been the preoccupation of the best minds of the East.[5]

What is this preoccupation of the Eastern mind? Jung puts it thus:

[4] *The Secret of the Golden Flower,* Richard Wilhelm's German translation rendered into English by Cary P. Baynes, pp. 95-96.
[5] *Ibid.,* pp. 82-83.

Because the things of the inner world influence us all the more powerfully for being unconscious it is essential for anyone who intends to make progress in self-culture to objectivate the effects of the anima and then try to understand what contents underlie those effects. In this way he adapts to, and is protected against, the invisible. No adaptation can result without concessions to both worlds.

From a consideration of the claims of the inner and outer worlds, or rather, from the conflicts between them, the possible and the necessary follows. Unfortunately our Western mind, lacking all culture in this respect, has never yet devised a concept, nor even a name, for the *union of opposites through the middle path,* that most fundamental item of inward experience, which could respectably be set against the Chinese concept of *Tao*.[6]

Never before has Chinese Taoism been so well explained in the light of modern psychology and sincerely pursued as a way to elevate man's mental activities and alleviate his sufferings. Thus the mystery of age-old Eastern wisdom, which brings out the best in man, is no longer a mystery but simply a way to wholesome and harmonious living.

Only thirty years later, in 1959, Joseph Needham of Cambridge University in his voluminous *Science and Civilization in China* (Vol. III) proves to us that Taoist philosophy was applied to astronomy and mathematics and that leading Taoists made contributions in geography, cartography, mineralogy, and chemistry. Based upon the Taoist theory of infinite empty space and the condensation of vapor, Chinese astronomers developed the *Hsüan Yeh* system, assuming that beyond the great circles of the celestial sphere there was infinite space. Needham's comment on this system is:

[6] C. G. Jung, *Collected Works,* Vol. III, "Two Essays on Analytical Psychology," translated from the German by R. F. G. Hull, p. 203.

The Hsüan Yeh system has a distinctive Taoist flavor, which may account for the disappearance of the oldest writings concerning it. One senses a connection with the "great emptiness" (*hsü wu*) of Lao Tzu, and with the idea of heaven as piled up chhi' (*chi chhi*) in Lieh Tzu. Significantly, most of what we know about it comes from Ko Hung and Li Shun-Feng.[7]

It is obvious that astronomy, which was a science of cardinal importance to the ancient Chinese, and a particular concern of the Taoist thinkers, had its roots in Taoist philosophy.

From Needham's work we also learn that the Taoist use of paradoxes gave inspiration to Chinese mathematicians. This contention is confirmed by an excerpt from an algebraist's commentary on another mathematician's book:

Heaven corresponds to the base of the right-angled triangle, earth to the height, man to the hypotenuse, and things to the diameter of a circle inscribed in the triangle, as may be seen from his diagrams. By moving the expressions upward and downward, and from side to side, by advancing and retiring, alternating and connecting, by changing, dividing and multiplying, by employing different signs for positive and negative, by keeping some and eliminating others and changing the positions of the counting-rods, by attacking from the front or from the side, as shown in the four examples—by not using (a thing) yet it is used; by not using a number the number required is obtained. Mathematicians aforetime could not attain the mysterious principles contained in the present profound book.[8]

This statement suggests that by the use of a number, or rather by its nonuse, the working out of equa-

[7] Joseph Needham, *Science and Civilization in China*, Vol. III, p. 221.
[8] *Ibid.*, p. 47.

tions and roots had become rather a philosophical than a mathematical proposition. Needham recognizes the Taoists' theory of the universality of change as one of their deep philosophical insights. The use of paradoxes by the mathematicians and the working theory of the astronomer of infinite empty space are evidence that Taoist thought was applied to natural science, and therewith another channel for the study of Taoism was opened up.

In the spring of 1952 when Jacques Maritain delivered a series of lectures at the National Gallery of Art in Washington he explained that the inner principle of dynamic harmony seized upon by Chinese contemplative artists should be conceived of as a "sort of interpenetration between Nature and Man." Through interpenetration things are spiritualized. When the artist reveals the reality concealed in things, he sets it free and, in turn, he liberates and purifies himself. This invisible process, fundamental to Chinese art, is the action of *Tao*. Maritain points out that there is a difference between Oriental and Occidental art: the former being intent on objectivity, the latter on subjectivity. However, at the root of their creative activity there is a common experience, without parallel in logical reason, by means of which objectivity and subjectivity are "obscurely grasped together." [9] It is the nondifferentiating awareness of creative intuition that gives his restatement of the basic principle of Chinese painting a fuller and richer meaning. "What does the first of the famous six canons of Hsieh Ho prescribe?—To have life-motion manifest the unique spiritual resonance that the artist

[9] Jacques Maritain, *Creative Intuition in Art and Poetry*, p. 84.

Plate 1   *Wu Wei* (1459–1508)
BRANCH OF PLUM BLOSSOMS

In this picture the artist signed his name as *Hsiao hsien Tzu,* or
"Master Similar to Immortals" by which he meant to say that the
spontaneity and simplicity of his brush-work resembled the work of
immortals. Once, when he was sent for by the court to paint a picture of "Pines and the Running Stream," he had not fully recovered
from his intoxication. When in front of the emperor, he inadvert-
ently knocked over the ink jar and some ink splashed on the silk.
Taking advantage of the splashed ink he made a wonderful drawing.
The admiring emperor sighed and said: "This is indeed the stroke
of an immortal."

Plate 2   *Huang Kung-wang* (1268–1354)
MANSION OF ORCHIDS

The colophon at the upper left corner is a poem composed and penned by the emperor Ch'ien-lung (1736–1796) of the Ch'ing dynasty, in which he compares Huang Kung-wang's paintings to Tu Fu's poetry.

Oftentimes I admire the poems of Tu Fu
In which he reveals spiritual reality.
Indeed, I love the talent of our ancient genius,
But do not overlook the greatness of the later artist.
Tai-ch'ih * has great love for men of talent.
His views must be the same as mine
Since he painted the Mansion of Orchids
As a token of his fondness for friendship.

Huang Kung-wang used to wander for days in the depth of the mountains, watching the play of light and shadow on the cliffs and peaks mornings and evenings. Sometimes he meditated in the deep bamboo grove and sometimes by the side of the roaring waves of the sea. Having penetrated into the nature of things he was able to bring out their spiritual reality in his brush-work.

The inscription by the artist says that the Great Innocence, the Taoist Huang Kung-wang, painted this picture when he was staying in the *Hsuan-chen Tao Tang,* or Mystic and Genuine Taoist Hall at Yünchien in the year 1342.

* *Tai-ch'ih* is the pen name of Huang Kung-wang, which means Great Innocence.

Plate 3   Attributed to Mi Fei (1051–1107)
MISTY LANDSCAPE: ROUND MOUNTAIN PEAKS AND TREES

This misty landscape is attributed to Mi Fei. The artist has broken away from traditional rules, using almost exclusively the ink wash to bring out objective reality of mountains, trees, and mists. Only a few light strokes are used for the temple roof. Although Mi Fei's ink wash was developed from Wang Hsia's splashing ink, his style is different from that of the Ch'an masters. In some of their works there is an overemphasis on appearance, called *pa han,* or overbearing audacity, by Chinese critics. Yin Yü-ch'ien, for instance, with his strong and bold strokes gives us a feeling of excessive force and swiftness. When contemplating Mi Fei's ink wash we get the feeling that something intangible emerges between the form and the formless, between the image and the imageless. The elusive and evasive qualities of his ink wash create that rarer atmosphere, as Laurence Binyon calls it, wherein the artist's inner serenity is released.

It is said that Mi Fei released his clothes and untied his belt when painting—even in the presence of the emperor. He not only used the hair brush but also the sponge of the lotus fruit, and sometimes the sugar cane after the juice had been pressed out.

Plate 4   Mu ch'i (active in 1269.
Pupil of priest Wu-chun, d. 1249)

SIX PERSIMMONS

Mu ch'i is the pen name of Fa chang, the Ch'an monk from Sze-
chuan. He was born in the early part of the thirteenth century. In
later years he stayed in the Liu-t'ung temple near Hangchow, where
the beautiful Western Lake is located. His landscape paintings are
done in ink wash, similar in style to Mi Fei's, but quite different
from the ink wash painting of Yin Yü-chien.

This picture of six persimmons is one of the best works ever produced by Chinese artists. Before Mu ch'i picked up his brush, his
mind was in the state of no-thought. Thus, we have in this painting
a manifestation of the primary indeterminacy of the uncarved block.
What his mind reflected at that moment his brush would put down.
First two deep black contours and then to their left two gray contours. To the extreme left and right he placed two plain white
contours. The ink wash of the two first contours is pitch dark without
any shading at all, and the two contours at the left are all gray with
only a light touch. The two outside contours are pure white. The
shades of the ink wash from dark to gray and from gray to white correspond to the inner process going on in the painter. When he was
still in the depth of the preconscious, the density of his creative
night found expression in two dark contours. With the awakening of
his consciousness, the inner darkness loses its density and manifests
in two gray contours. As he awakens fully, his creative innocence is
entirely unveiled. So the white contours are its expression. What is
expressed in the picture corresponds to what happened in his mind.
Through his brush-work, the various states of his mind can be traced
from the primary indeterminacy of the uncarved block to transparency.

Bearing in mind that Mu ch'i was primarily a Ch'an monk, we can
well understand his supreme achievement in art, which is far beyond
mere technical perfection.

Plate 5   Shih t'ao '(1641-c. 1717)

TREES AND ROCK BANK

This picture was painted for the nephew of Shih t'ao, a young aspiring artist. The colophon states that the master expounded the first principle of painting, which is based upon the *Ch'an* Buddhist philosophy, and then gave a demonstration of it in his brush-work of "bare essentials." The term "bare essentials" was given by my friend who was able to appreciate this picture. It is through these "bare essentials" that the primary indeterminacy is revealed.

The following poem reflects Shih t'ao's serenity:

My primordial nature has no liking for the life in the cities.
To be free from the noise I built a little thatched cottage
Far away in the depth of the mountains.
Wandering here and there I carry no thought.
When spring comes I watch the birds;
In summer I bathe in the running stream;
In autumn I climb the highest peaks;
During the winter I am warming up in the sun.
Thus I enjoy the real flavor of the seasons.
Let the sun and the moon revolve by themselves!
When I have time I read the sutras,
When I am tired I sleep on my straw bed.
If you ask me, "Whom do you see in your dreams?"
I would answer, "The Yellow Emperor." *
It was he who transmitted the secret teaching to me,
Which I am forbidden to pass on to you.
I have worn the black robe now for decades.
The meaning of the teaching is profound and vast like the ocean.
When I reveal it in my brush-work, its merits are limitless.
Should I explain this secret teaching to you
The solid mountain, I am afraid, would blow away.

* The earliest Taoist ruler according to legend.

論畫者如論禪相似貴不
存如解入第一義方為
高手否則即謂第二義
矣絕非敷衍雨腿卒耕
隱但論畫郤書此紙　石濤濟

Plate 6   Ni Tsan (1301–1374)
BAMBOO BRANCH

Ni Tsan painted this picture on the sixth day of the second month in the year of *chia yin* (1374), the last year of his life. He gave it to Wu hsüeh, the abbot of the monastery where he stayed. At the upper right-hand corner is a poem written by a friend, a comment on the bamboo branch:

It is like scattered drops of rain wrestling outside the window;
Or like blue clouds emerging from the rocks.
Who else but Master Ni Tsan can produce such purity?

Osvald Siren makes the following statement on Ni Tsan's work:

Ni Tsan did not lean on the models of early Sung times to the same extent as most of his contemporaries, nor did he become the head of a school or local group. Yet, with the passing of time his highly individualistic art came to have a considerable influence on later generations of landscape painters. The leading critics at the end of the Ming and the beginning of the Ch'ing period never tired of extolling him as primus inter pares, i.e., the most exquisite and refined of all the Yuan masters.

The secret of the significance of his art was, according to these expounders, something that could not be adequately described in words or rendered in copies, however skillfully made; they are alluring through their apparent simplicity and freedom from all traditional elements of decorative beauty or elaboration. Somehow they seemed to reveal a singularly attractive, yet unattainable spirit of aloofness or detachedness, a genius for whom the stones and the trees and the mountain ranges beyond the quiet water were simply symbols for his meditative moods and deepest thoughts.

Nothing could be more unassuming, more restful and quiet than Ni Tsan's river views with a few leafless trees or bamboo stalks on a rocky bank or islet, yet they transmitted a state of meditative repose and comprehension of the soul of nature that no one else could evoke with such simple means. It exercised a singular attraction on kindred talents among later painters of kindred disposition, who did their utmost to imitate Ni Tsan's seemingly plain and artless works but hardly ever succeeded in transmitting their inmost beauty or spiritual reverberation (*Chinese Painting*, Vol. IV, p. 79).

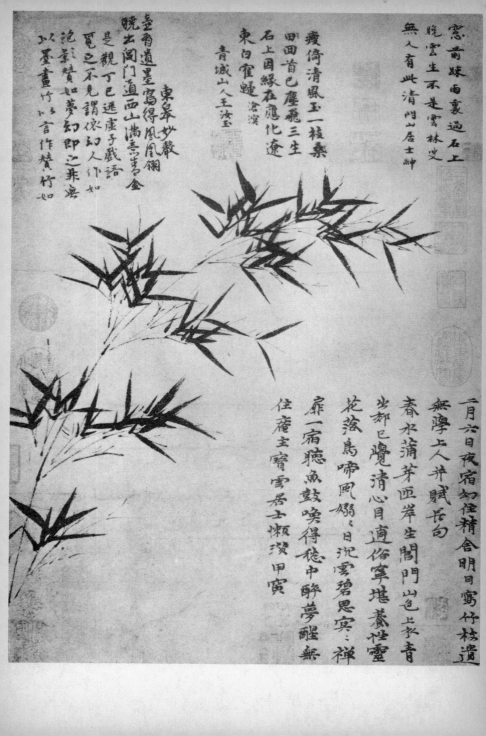

Plate 7   T'ang Mi *(1668–1739)*

BAMBOO TREES

This picture was painted by T'ang Mi in the year 1726 in Nantung,
the town beside five hills on the northern bank of the Yangtzu River
mouth, where I myself was born. T'ang Mi was a scholar and painter,
who specialized in bamboo and birds. He knew how to bring out the
actuality of things. This beautiful picture gives us the impression that
real bamboo trees are growing out of the rocks. Although there is
delicacy and refinement in his brush-work, it cannot match the bamboos painted by Ni Tsan, which live and thrive in the atmosphere of
inner serenity. His minute work, as seen in the intricately interwoven
little twigs and leaves, shows his devotion to faithful imitation of
externalities.

Plate 8 *Wang Tseng-tsu*
BAMBOO TREES

To the Chinese the bamboo tree is the symbol of the gentleman because of its upright outward bearing and its inner emptiness, which he interprets as humbleness. Traditionally there are three friends among the trees that endure the bristling cold together during the late winter: the pine, the bamboo, and the plum.

This painting is the work of a less known artist, a specialist of bamboo. It shows the plant standing upright in a heavy snow storm, with one branch broken off and the rest of the branches covered with snow. This picture may be taken for a symbolic expression of the painter's own subjective ideality.

Plate 9   Shih t'ao (1641-c. 1717)
POET AND PINES

This picture reflects Shih t'ao's inner tranquillity. The poet who strolls on top of the hill under the needles of the pine trees is his symbolized self.

The poem in the upper left corner, composed by him, reveals his inner serenity:

What does the old master do here?
By the side of the rock he is hunting for a new verse.
Suddenly a cool breeze blows from the pine tree;
Silently and quietly it purifies his spirit and thought.

In the simplicity of the pine branches and the figure of the poet we feel the transparency of Shih t'ao's brush-work.

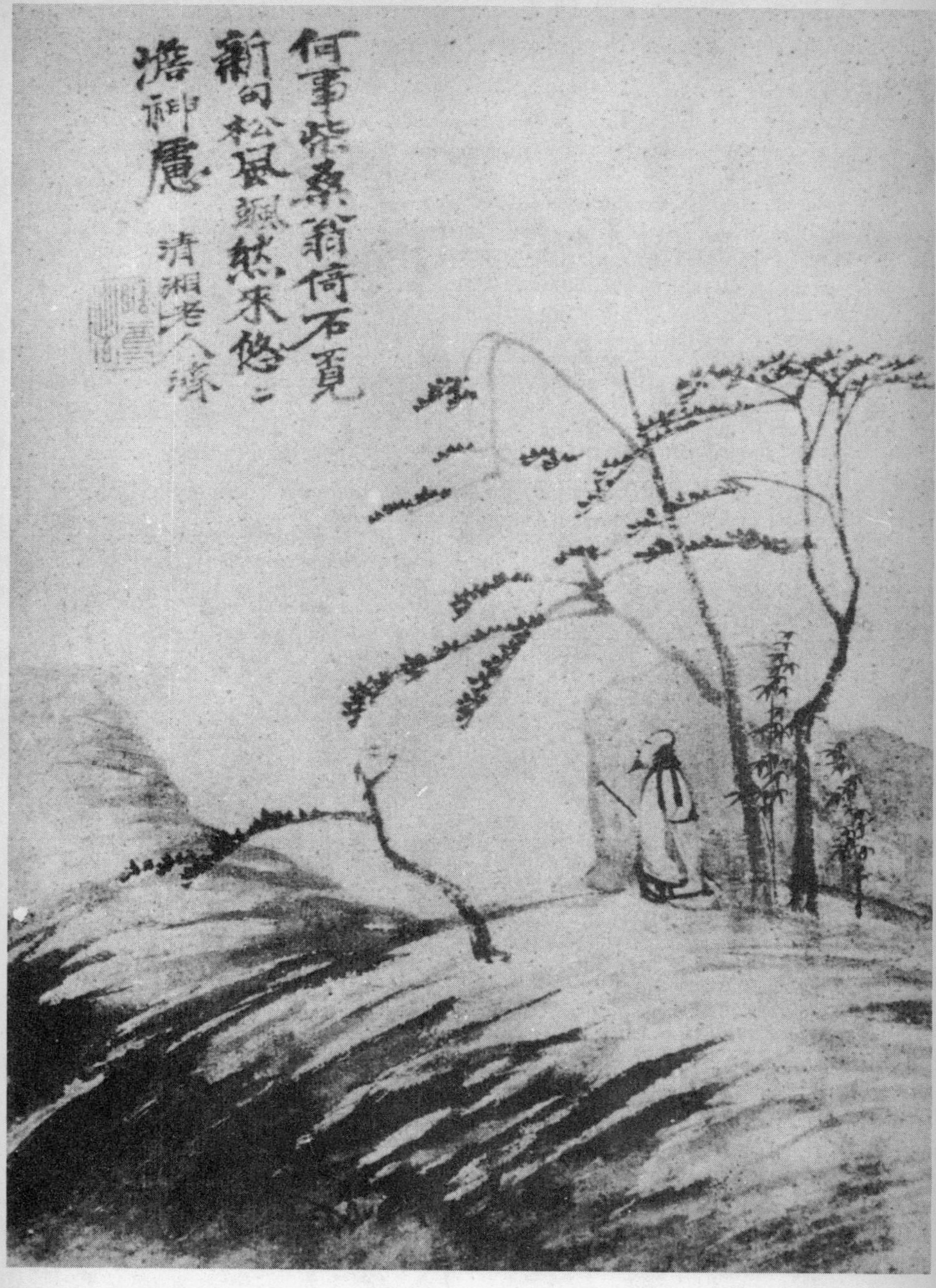
何事柴桑翁倚石覓
新句松風飄然來悠悠
浩神慮
清湘老人濟

Plate 10   Pa-ta Shan-jen (1626-c. 1701)

FLOWER IN VASE

This painting is done in broad sweeping strokes. The artist's brush, unhampered in its action by confining conventional rules, is carefree and at ease. No attempt is made at beauty or refinement of form; merely the primary essentials of the objects are given. Here we see innocence or the quality of the uncarved block at its best. What is within is manifested without.

In one of his calligraphic writings Pa-ta Shan-jen says:

When the mind is transparent and pure as if reflected on the mirror-like surface of the water, there is nothing in the world that you would dislike. When it is serene as the light breeze in the sunshine, there will be no one whom you would like to forget.

The following part of a letter written to him by Shih t'ao reads:

Master, you are now close to seventy-four years old and yet you climb the mountains as if flying on wings. You must indeed be one of the immortals!

May I ask you to paint a scroll for me about three feet by one foot? Please draw several small houses on the slope of a hill surrounded by old trees, and in one of them an old man to represent me staying in my thatched hut. Should there be space for writing, kindly add some calligraphy of yours, which would make it a most valued treasure of mine.

In his calligraphy Pa-ta Shan-jen followed the style of Mi Fei who, as mentioned before, was one of the great Taoist painters.

Plate 11   Ch'i Pai-shih (1861–1957)
COW AND WILLOWS

Some long undulating lines, a monochrome contour, and a few small light strokes make up the composition of the picture. The long wavy lines represent willow trees. We can feel their swaying motion in the summer breeze. In contrast to this carefree motion there is calmness centered in the monochrome contour of a cow. The eyes, horns, and the mouth are done with dark strokes. The simple and calm nature of the cow is well expressed. With big innocent eyes she gazes into the distance. The tail, just one strong black line, suggests slight motion of the cow's body. The small horizontal lines are swallows playing gaily in the high sky.

There is a well-balanced combination of movement and calmness in the picture. The atmosphere throughout is of rare transparency. When the artist held the brush his innermost being must have been tranquil and serene.

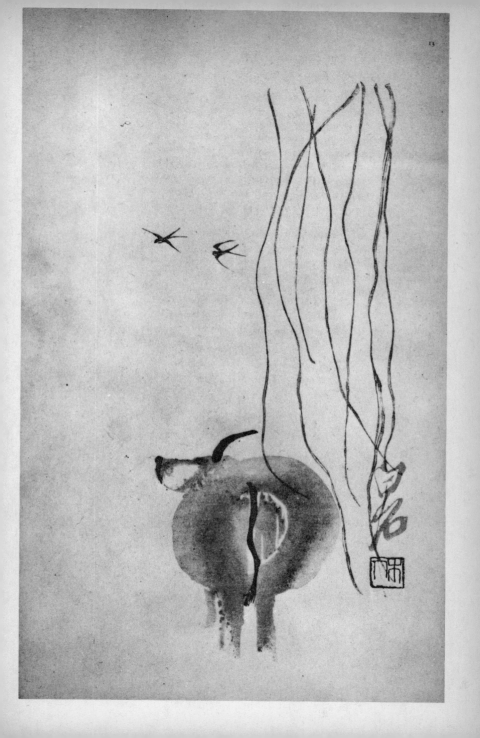

Plate 12　　*Ch'i Pai-shih* *(1861–1957)*
BAMBOO BRANCH

This bamboo painting has qualities of its own which set it apart from the three previous selections.

Plate 7 by T'ang Mi expresses the actual beauty of the bamboo, its graceful elegance, which is pleasing to the eye. Plate 8 is composed of a number of strong strokes, which bring out the strength and endurance traditionally attributed to the bamboo. Here we have an ideological projection from the painter to the object painted. Plate 6 by Ni Tsan is suffused with Heavenly radiance. The delicate stems and the wide openings between the leaves impart a feeling of lightness.

This painting has neither objective beauty, nor subjective ideality, nor Heavenly radiance. Instead, here the qualities of the uncarved block are in evidence. The simple blunt strokes are a direct revelation from the unconscious. Because he tapped its depth he achieved greatness in his work. When we look for instance at his drawing of an empty dish, done with only three circles, we get indeed the feeling of emptiness or the void, and we can well understand his prediction made in the inscription: "Those who like this picture will in future be known."

catches in Things, inspired as he is by his communion with the spirit of the cosmos." [10]

When Maritain expounds the notion of harmonious expansion, he relates it to the Chinese concept *k'ai ho,* or unity of coherence, by quoting a leading Chinese artist:

> Where things grow and expand that is *k'ai;* where things are gathered up, that is *ho.* When you expand (*k'ai*) you should think of gathering up (*ho*) and then there will be structure; when you gather up (*ho*) you should think of expanding (*k'ai*) and then you will have inexpressible effortlessness and an air of inexhaustible spirit. In using the brush and in laying out the composition, there is not a moment when you can depart from *k'ai-ho.*[11]

This principle of *k'ai-ho,* or expanding and gathering up, which is based upon Taoist paradoxes, says Maritain, is universally applied by both Oriental and Occidental artists because it is essential to the structure of a painting.

From the foregoing, it follows that ever since the beginning of the nineteenth century Taoist ideas have flown like an invisible stream into the mind of the West, to scholars who held differing views concerning *Tao* and whose insight was applied to their respective subjects. Besides the thinkers mentioned above there have been many other men and women of learning deeply interested in the philosophy of *Tao* and who have applied its wisdom to their studies. We may say that these manifestations are the "countenance of the Great Achievement" of which Lao Tzu speaks in the *Tao Te Ching:*

[10] *Ibid.,* p. 14.
[11] *Ibid.,* p. 337. The unity of coherence is also observed by George Rowley in his book, *Principles of Chinese Painting.*

The countenance of the Great Achievement
is simply a manifestation of Tao.
That which is called Tao
is indistinct and ineffable.
Ineffable and indistinct,
yet therein are forms.
Indistinct and ineffable
yet therein are objects.
Deep-seated and unseen,
therein are essences.
The essence is quite real,
therein is the vivid Truth (Ch. XXI).

Although *Tao* is indistinct and ineffable, latent in it
are forms and objects. Those who penetrate into the
deep-seated and unseen reveal the essence of *Tao*.
From the application of Taoist philosophy to psychology, natural science, and art, we see that the essence of *Tao* is evident.

Not only did Taoist thought pave the way for advancement of Chinese art, science, mathematics, and
psychology, but many centuries ago some of its basic
principles flowed together with other schools of philosophy, notably Buddhism and Confucianism. In the
beginning of the fifth century the great Indian teacher
Kumārajīva directed the work of translating and exe-
getizing the Buddhist texts into Chinese. One of his
students and fellow workers, Seng-chao (384-414),
composed a famous work, referred to as *The Book of
Chao,* in which he expounded Buddhism in terms of
Taoism. In his first chapter, "On the Immutability of
Things," Seng-chao maintains that action and nonaction are not isolated, but coalescent. Things in action are simultaneously forever in nonaction; things
in nonaction are forever in action. Thus nonaction

does not mean quiescence after action has ceased, but quiescence forever in action. Seng-chao contends that even though Heaven and Earth were suddenly to change their positions we could not say that they were not in nonaction, or even though breakers were to rush heavenward, we could not say that they were in action. Seng-chao's identification of action and non-action corresponds to what Chuang Tzu says in the chapter entitled "The Identity of All Things": "This is also that; that is also this," and "Destruction is construction; construction is destruction. There is no destruction or construction. They fuse into one." When we do not assert either action or nonaction, this or that, being or nonbeing, we are free from both. In the expression of the Buddhist, we are following the Middle Path, which, as I see it, is the same concept that Lao Tzu refers to when he says, "Being and nonbeing create each other," and "The wise follow the path of non-assertion and teach without words" (*Ch. II*). The idea of interfusion and identification of opposites such as being and nonbeing, action and nonaction, so much in evidence in the second chapter of the *Chuang Tzu* and in the *Tao Te Ching,* is often used by Buddhists to expound their *sutras.*

Another idea shared by both Buddhism and Taoism is that unity is within diversities and the particularity is identified with universality. Fa tsang (643-712), the founder of a school known as Hua yen (Wreath) Buddhism, expounding the metaphor of Indra's net, points out the basic idea of mutual and simultaneous penetration of one in all and all in one. Thus one is all, and all is one. His teaching reminds us strongly of the Taoist principle of unity within diversities. In his commentary on "Identity of All Things," the second chapter of the *Chuang Tzu,* Chang T'ai-yen identifies Fa tsang's ideas with those of Chuang Tzu. He quotes Fa tsang's words from *The Original Meaning of the Avatamaska:* "The petal of a blossom never comes forth alone, but unimpededly takes in all related parts of the blooming tree," and "This petal must dissolve itself, thus entering into all and taking in all" (*Section II*).

Chang T'ai-yen maintains that this idea of Fa tsang is the same as that of Chuang Tzu when he says:

Why I like to divide things is because such division must be based upon the totality of things. The creation of one rests upon the all. Why I dislike to complete things is because completeness means containing everything. Therefore it is isolated and self-sufficient, rejecting the relation to other things (*Ch. XXIII*).

From this analysis by Chang T'ai-yen we see that some ideas of Taoist and Buddhist thought often coalesce.

The third idea of Taoism shared by Chinese Buddhism is *tzu jan,* or self-so-ness, the naturalness and spontaneity of things. It cannot be reached by intellection. Our minds are awakened to it, rather, by themselves. Such self-realization requires no artificial effort. The Taoist speaks of *wu wei,* or noninterference. To Chinese *Ch'an* (*Zen* in Japanese) the best method of cultivating Buddhahood is noncultivation. To cultivate one's mind is to exercise deliberate effort, *yu wei,* the opposite of *wu wei.* The sixth patriarch, Hui neng, maintains that the Buddha nature is within you, and that all you have to do to find it is to realize it. This idea is incorporated in the famous saying, "The ordinary mind is *Tao*." The ordinary mind is spontaneous self-so-ness, which is also the basic teaching of Taoism. Tracing the history of *Ch'an* Buddhism, we find that it is practically a further development of the early philosophy of Lao Tzu and Chuang Tzu.

Chinese scholars maintain that the revolutionary idea on enlightenment held by *Ch'an* Buddhism should be traced back as far as the fourth century, when Tao-sheng (ca. 360-434) attacked the traditional theory of gradual attainment and instead advocated the theory of sudden enlightenment. He said:

Words convey ideas. When ideas have been absorbed words cease. . . . Only those who can take the fish and forget the net are worthy to seek *Tao*.[12]

With this statement Tao-sheng almost quotes Chuang Tzu:

The fishing net is used to catch fish; let us have the fish and forget the net. The snare is used to catch rabbits; let us have the rabbit and forget the snare. Words are used to convey ideas; let us have the ideas and forget the words.[13]

Tao-sheng's revolutionary idea of sudden enlightenment paved the way for the development of *Ch'an* Buddhism. His explanation of this viewpoint was obviously influenced by Chuang Tzu's philosophy.

A hundred years before Tao-sheng applied Taoist principles to an explanation of the Buddhist enlight-

[12] *Kao Seng Chuan,* or *Biographies of Eminent Buddhist Monks,* Vol. V, p. 366.
[13] *Works of Chuang Tzu,* Ch. XXVI.

enment, Wang Pi (226-249) was using the same idea in interpreting Confucianist classics. In his commentary on the *I Ching,* or *Book of Changes,* he thrust aside the traditional interpretation of the *I Ching* as "the study of emblems and numbers," and instead proclaimed that the great emblem has no form even as the great *Tao* has no name. When the idea is obtained the emblem is forgotten. Wang Pi says:

Words are used to explain emblems. When the emblem is understood, words are forgotten. Emblems are used to convey ideas. When ideas are grasped, emblems are forgotten. This is the same as when we say that the snare serves to catch the rabbit. When the rabbit is obtained the snare is forgotten. The fish net serves to catch the fish. When the fish is obtained the net is forgotten.[14]

Wang Pi further says of the *I Ching:*

When the line can express the idea of compliance there is no need to identify the trigram *K'un* with a cow; when the line can express firmness, there is no need to identify the trigram *Ch'ien* with a horse. Thus one would keep the idea and forget the symbol.[15]

According to Wang Pi, any of the lines in a given hexagram can become the dominant factor or the supreme solitary one. One is the beginning of the numbers and the ultimate of things. Chuang Tzu says: "That which is one is one, and that which is not-one is also one." The solitary one of Wang Pi is also not-one, which means nonbeing, or *Wu*. Since one is the source of all numbers, it is said to be not a number but that from which all numbers are formed. Thus

[14] Wang Pi, *Chou Yi Lueh-li,* or *Outline of the System Used in Chou Changes,* Section II, "Understanding Emblems."
[15] *Ibid.*

what is one is *Wu,* or Nonbeing, which is also identified with the ultimate. Because it is the origin of all things, it is called *T'ai Chi,* or the supreme ultimate—or *Tao.*

The above interpretations of Confucian classics shows the influx of Taoist ideas. T'ang Yung-t'ung says:

> In the Han dynasty Ching Chiao's study of the *I Ching* concentrated on emblems and numbers. . . . Wang Pi disliked the former's artificial methods which extend even to the five elements, deviating thereby more and more from the original meaning. Wang Pi speaks of great *Tao* as emptiness and selflessness, hence he advocated the real Oneness, the forgetting of words and symbols, the experience of the mystic Ultimate. . . . Thus we see that Confucianism, which had been so strong during the Han dynasty, ceased to be attractive and its place was taken by Neo-Taoism.[16]

The interpretation of the Confucian classics by Taoism, as in the work of Wang Pi, was only the beginning of the process of synthesis. Neo-Confucianism, as represented in the work of Chou Tun-yi (1017-1073) and Chu Hsi (1130-1200) which came into flower in later dynasties, had a very strong overtone of Taoist thought.

I have presented here some of the manifestations of *Tao* as it occurs in different fields and have briefly discussed its fusion into various schools of Chinese Buddhism and Confucianism. This is intended merely as a background to the understanding of the philosophy of Taoism as it was originated in the works of Lao Tzu and Chuang Tzu. In the first three chapters of

16 T'ang Yung-t'ung, *History of Buddhism in Han, Wei Chin, and in the Period of Disunity,* Vol. II, p. 630.

this book, dealing with sympathy, creativity, and peace, I have made an attempt to present Taoist ideas in a systematic way—although *Tao* itself is inexpressible. The chapters on poetry and painting are intended to show how the invisible *Tao* manifests itself through art. The chapter on self-realization points out ways of self cultivation toward the ultimate goal of enlightenment.

Most of the ideas incorporated in this book were first presented in different form in lectures at Oxford University; the Royal Institute of Philosophy, London; the C. G. Jung Institute, Zurich; the Eranos Congress, Ascona, Switzerland; and the XIIth International Congress of Philosophy, Venice. The first three chapters, which have appeared in the *Eranos Yearbooks,* have undergone a number of changes. The chapter on self-realization was rewritten from a paper entitled "An Introduction to Taoist Yoga," which was published in the *Review of Religion,* Columbia University.

In presenting this little work to my readers I want to express my deep gratitude to Professor Daisetz T. Suzuki, from whom I have learned much that I could not have learned from anyone else, and who in turn accepted my ideas as no one else could have accepted them. Professor C. G. Jung clarified my understanding of *Tao* in the light of modern scientific psychology. Professor Leo Robertson, Director of the Royal Institute of Philosophy, wrote me after he had read my paper on creativity, and said that my interpretation of creativity was a contribution to the field. The chapter on poetry was read with keen interest by both Professor Jacques Maritain and Sir Herbert Read. The latter wrote me to say that "to relate Chinese poetry to a philosophical background very much increases its significance for English readers." The chapter on painting was carefully read by Professor Jane Mahler of Columbia University, whose suggestions have been of great help.

Finally, I am most grateful to the Bollingen Foundation, whose assistance enabled me to devote my time to a thorough study of Taoist philosophy and to the development of some basic ideas which are so fundamental to Chinese culture that I have tried to put forward here. The insight and good will that the executive of the Foundation showed me are worthwhile mentioning and extremely valuable for the scholar's work in the present-day world.

1 Invisible ground of sympathy

The understanding of *Tao* is an inner experience in which distinction between subject and object vanishes. It is an intuitive, immediate awareness rather than a mediated, inferential, or intellectual process. *Tao* does not blossom into vital consciousness until all distinctions between self and nonself have disappeared. T'ao Ch'ien of the fourth century has described this experience in the following verse:

I gather chrysanthemums at the eastern hedgerow
And silently gaze at the southern mountains.
The mountain air is beautiful in the sunset,
And the birds flocking together return home.
Among all these things is a real meaning,
Yet when I try to express it, I become lost in "no-words."

In this poem, when T'ao Ch'ien looks at the mountains, the birds, the flowers, and the setting sun, we have an initial differentiation between the seer and the objects seen. But when the poet penetrates into the reality of all these things, a unity, a oneness, is immediately achieved. Subject and object are mutually identified. At this stage the poet's self is dissolved in the realm of no-words. Su Tung-p'o of the eleventh century commented, "the delight of reading the poem lies in the fact that suddenly, without purpose, the poet's mind and his surroundings are unified, as he gazes at the mountains while picking flowers." This inner experience of interfusion of subject and object may be illustrated by a famous story from the works of Chuang Tzu:

Once I dreamt that I was a butterfly, fluttering here and there; in all ways a butterfly. I enjoyed my freedom as a butterfly, not knowing that I was Chou. Suddenly I awoke and was surprised to be myself again. Now, how can I tell whether I was a man who dreamt that he was a butterfly, or whether I am a butterfly who dreams that she is a man? Between Chuang Chou and the butterfly, there must be differentiation. [Yet in the dream nondifferentiation takes place.] This is called interfusion of things (*Ch. II*).

In this story Chuang Tzu dreams of a butterfly. Chuang Tzu, thus, is the subject and the butterfly is the object. But, he says, it might be that the butterfly was dreaming of itself as a man, making the butterfly the subject and the man, Chuang Tzu himself, the object. Is it possible to make a distinction here between subject and object? The awareness of the identification and interpenetration of self and nonself is the key that unlocks the mystery of *Tao*.

Before the introduction of Buddhism to China there were at least two basic concepts of sympathy in Chinese thought. One was the Confucianist ideal of fellow-feeling, proceeding from the self to the selves of others. It is the process of expansion from the egocentric consciousness to the consciousness of one's fellow men. The individual expanded his love about him in gradated quantities, beginning with his relatives, extending to other persons, and ultimately penetrating and embracing the "ten thousand things." The second of the pre-Buddhist concepts of sympathy in China is found in the views of the Taoists. This sympathy was primordial identification, interfusion, and unification of subject and object, of one and many, of man and the universe. It was not a product of rational intellection, but an ontological experience.

While I wish to concentrate on the concept of sympathy as we find it in Taoist thought, it may be helpful first to consider the Confucianist point of view for the sake of the light cast by the comparison.

The Confucianist term *Jen* is often translated as "love," "fellow-feeling," "man-to-man-ness," and many others. The word *Jen* embodies the central theme of Confucianist thought. This sympathy is based on rational discrimination and differentiation. Mencius (371?-289? B.C.), the Plato of China, claims that *"Jen* is the mind of man." What is this mind of man? It is the rational nature of man, the conscious ability of discrimination and determination of things. The entire system of Confucianism is based upon the premise of man's rational nature. The first step toward the achievement of this rational nature is the performance of one's moral duty. Such imperative, unconditioned action, which is beyond self-interest and ulterior motive, is called *yi,* or righteousness. If one does what he ought to do and does not do what he should not do, he is abiding by the virtue of righteousness. However, one's concept of duty is not without personal bias. One may act in one way, and another may act in another way. What would be the correct response to the same situation? To clarify this point the Confucianist set a standard of conduct to determine what righteousness is, which is called *li*, or propriety. This standard of conduct covers all types of interpersonal relations and all ceremonies of worship.

But within the framework of propriety questions arise as to how we must apply the rules. When new circumstances arise we must use our judgment in applying general rules. In the Confucianist term this judgment of what is proper and what is improper is called *chih*, or wisdom, by which is meant the ability of discrimination. Mencius puts it this way:

When there is choice between taking a thing and not taking it, to take it is contrary to moderation. When there is choice between giving a thing and not giving it, to give it is contrary to kindness. When there is choice between sacrificing one's life and not sacrificing it, to sacrifice it is contrary to bravery.[1]

To determine whether one's action is correct or incorrect, or whether it appears proper and actually is improper, one cannot follow blindly the rules or *li*. What one must have is the ability of discrimination or *chih*.[2] Confucius says: "The man of *chih* is free from confusion." Thus rational discrimination is the fundamental process leading to the achievement of *jen*. In it is implied the measuring out of one's love. How much love, the Confucianist asks, does one owe to rela-

[1] *The Works of Mencius,* Book IV, Section II, translated by James Legge.
[2] *Chih,* when used by the Confucianists, means rational conscious knowledge; when used by the Taoists and Buddhists, it has the meaning of intuitive knowledge.

tives, other men, and all things? The exact gradations have been expressed in a clear formulation by Mencius:

> As to animals the gentleman is kind but not loving. As to persons generally he is loving but not affectionate. He is affectionate to his parents and lovingly disposed to people generally. He is lovingly disposed to people generally, and kind to animals (*Book VII, Section II*).

This gradation of sympathy creates positions of superiority and inferiority and relations of nearness and remoteness. As a man becomes more superior, he becomes more remote. Superiority and remoteness are in a positive correlation. The effect of differentiation is to make vain the hope of direct, immediate fellow-feeling between men. At its worst, Confucianism is a sterile effort to carry out a system. Too often, in the process, the primordial warmth originally connoted by *Jen* is lost. This is evident in the works of the two great legalists of the third century B.C., Han Fei and Li Ssu. The legalistic system of gradation, based on the teaching of the great Confucianist Hsün Ch'ing (ca. 298 to ca. 238 B.C.), represents the extreme development of so-called "rational" sympathy.

Because of the artificiality and coldness that *Jen* tended to create and the remoteness and isolation it engendered, the Taoists often declared that they would banish *Jen* so that the people could once again love one another. Lao Tzu felt this way and Chuang Tzu expressed himself even more strongly, declaring that it was necessary to get rid of *Jen* so that the virtue of the people might become one with God.

Lao Tzu disregarded *Jen* and proclaimed that he

had, instead, *Tz'u*, the first of his "three treasures." The word *Tz'u* is ordinarily translated as love, but it is not actually love itself but, rather, the primordial, immediate source of love, the secret root of all love and compassion. It is not based on rational principles or arrived at through discrimination and differentiation. On the contrary, it is intuitively and unconsciously arrived at and nothing, good or evil, is distinguished or extended. Through *Tz'u* subject and object are totally and immediately interfused and the self is transformed into selflessness. When the Buddhists came to China they used the words *Tz'u* and *Pei* (sorrow) to render the idea of great compassion. They did not use the word *Jen*. It is obvious that the Taoist concept of *Tz'u* is that of great sympathy. Their concept of love goes deeper than the concept of *Jen*.

In order to understand the nature of the great sympathy according to Taoism we must first investigate the basic meaning of *Tao*. To begin with, *Tao* literally signifies way or road. In the oldest form in which we find the character it appears thus: 𝍐 , comprised of three elements, representing respectively a road, 彳, a human head, 𝍐, and a human foot, 𝍐 . The manner in which the hair on the head is arranged indicates that it is the head of a leader. The foot suggests a follower. It would be incorrect, in my view, to interpret the head and foot together as a symbol for an individual man, since the very simple character still used for man, 𝍐 , appears on the oracle bones that long antedate the bronzes. Rather, we may rea-

sonably interpret this symbol as signifying a leader
and follower united in finding their path.

In collections of bronze inscriptions[3] we find the
ideograph of *Tao* variously depicted, as for instance
on a *p'an* (large vase) of the San family in the early
Chou Dynasty (about 11th century B.C.). Ordinarily
the symbol is composed of three elements, as mentioned above: road, head, and foot. Here we have a
clear indication of the unit signifying a leader and
follower searching their path. We also find a number
of similar combinations on oracle bones as early as
1400 B.C.: deer-chase, pig-chase, dog-chase, hare-chase,
and the like. Each of these ideographs is made up of
two elements. The upper element in each case represents the animal involved and the lower a human foot,
the chaser. One of these combinations, the pig-chase,
has persisted to the present day in the general sense
of chase. Hence we may logically infer the meaning of
foot as follower. In the ideograph of *Tao*, instead of a
man following an animal, one man follows another,
presumably a leader.

In pre-Confucian China the word *Tao* had already
become implicitly and explicitly a symbol of the ideals
of men. In the *Shu Ching* we find, "Heaven cannot be
trusted. Our Way (*Tao*) is merely to seek the prolon-
gation of the virtue of the Tranquilizing King." That
is, trust in the virtue of the great leader. As the word
Tao had intrinsic power in the philosophy of various
schools, such as those identified with Lao Tzu, Confucius, Mo Tzu, Yang Tzu, and others, all took ad-

[3] Such as those of Liu Hsin-yuan, *Ch'i Ku Shih Chi Chin Wen Shu*
(*Description of the Bronze Inscription*), (1902) VIII, 21 f., and M. J.
Kuo, *Liang Chou Chin Wen Tz'u Ta Hsi Tu Lu* (*Plates of Systems
of the Bronze Writing in Two Chou Dynasties*), Tokyo, 1937, 127.

vantage of the potency of the word and seized upon it for use in their respective systems. In the last chapter of the *Works of Chuang Tzu,* "The World," the author remarks:

There are many masters in the schools of philosophy in the world of today. Each of them claims to have found the correct answer. When we ask, "Where is the philosophy of the ancient *Tao?*" we may answer, "It is in every system."

On the other hand, the Confucianist Hsün Ch'ing maintains that none of these schools taught the *Tao* of the ancients correctly. He says:

If we look upon *Tao* as utility, we are merely seeking profit. If we look upon *Tao* as desire, we are merely seeking satisfaction. If we look upon *Tao* as law, we are merely gaining a technique. If we look upon *Tao* as power, we are merely seeking convenience. If we look upon *Tao* as words, we are merely being dialectic. If we look upon *Tao* as nature, we are merely finding cause and effect. These different presentations are all one particular aspect of *Tao.*[4]

Because the word *Tao* acquired powerful overtones we find adherents of all the early philosophic and religious schools adopting the term and attempting to explain it according to their tenets. Even the Buddhists, when they came to China in the first century A.D., declared that *Tao* is the road that leads to Nirvana. The Chinese Buddhists translated the Indian *Eightfold Noble Truth* with *Pa Sheng Tao.* The Bodhi Tree, under which Buddha attained enlightenment, is called *Tao Shu,* or the Tree of *Tao.* Buddhist philosophy was reinterpreted in China in terms of

[4] *The Works of Hsün Tzu,* Book XXI.

Taoist philosophy, and this practice resulted in a remarkable fusion of Indian Buddhism with Taoism and led to the formation of the Chinese form of Buddhism. Nan-ch'üan P'u-yuan (784-834), a well-known Buddhist Master, once said: "The *Tao* is not classifiable as either knowledge or nonknowledge . . . it is like a wide expanse of emptiness." Thus, all seeking the Nirvana of endless emptiness are working toward their conception of *Tao*. However, according to Nan-ch'üan, the *Tao*, does not end with Enlightenment of Nirvana, but man still has the tasks of daily life to perform as an essential part of his experience of *Tao*. There is among the Ch'anists the saying, "In carrying water and chopping wood—therein lies the wonderful *Tao*." The early Chinese Buddhist monks were referred to generally as *Tao jen*, or men of *Tao*. According to Chinese history, many celebrated Buddhist monks incorporated the word *Tao* into their names: Tao-an (A.D. 312-385), Tao-sheng (died A.D. 434), Tao-hsin (A.D. 580-636), Tao-i (Ma-Tsu) (died 788), etc. For centuries the word *Tao* has been interpreted and worshiped by the Chinese Buddhists.

The concept of *Tao* originated by early philosophers was expanded in the Taoist religion proper. According to tradition Taoism as a philosophy was established by Lao Tzu and Chuang Tzu in the period between the sixth century and the fourth century B.C. The ritualism of Taoism was first extensively organized by Chang Ling (later known as Chang Tao Ling) in the first century A.D. Thereafter, much energy and time were expended on the development and observation of formalistic ritual and regiments for attaining immortality. Much attention was devoted to the for-

mulation and use of magical spells and charms. Therefore the *Tao* was distorted and mostly degenerated
into a form of magic power and superstition. In the
fourth century A.D. Ko Hung further developed the
alchemical and ritualistic aspects of Taoism to the further neglect of the philosophy of the founders, and
they began using mysterious potions for an extension
of man's natural life span. In our day Christian mis-
sionaries have availed themselves of the force inherent in the word. Thus the earliest translation of the
Gospel according to St. John reads: "In the beginning
was the *Tao* and the *Tao* was with God, and the *Tao*
was God." Even the religious devotees from the Western world adopted *Tao* as the name for their divinity.
Thus it is evident that the *Tao* played an important
role in the life and culture of the Chinese, as various
schools of philosophy and religions adopted this term.

Of course, the *Tao* that I am going to discuss in this
book is chiefly exemplified in the works of Lao Tzu
and Chuang Tzu. But before I expound the meaning
of *Tao*, I would like to review briefly the authorship
of *Tao Te Ching*, which has been a great issue among
Chinese scholars during the last hundred and fifty
years.

Traditionally, the book was believed to have been
written by Lao Tan, or Old Tan, whose real name
was Li Erh, a man some twenty years older than Confucius. But late in the eighteenth century a Chinese
scholar named Wang Chung (1745-1794) challenged
this traditional concept and attributed the authorship
to a historian named Tai Shih Tan, of the Chou Dynasty. Shortly thereafter other scholars declared that
the *Tao Te Ching* must have been written some time

between the fourth and third centuries B.C., since the
work contains considerable discussion of the problem
name vs. nameless. It follows from the latter that it
must have been contemporaneous with the work of
the philosophers of the School of Names, which flour-
ished under the leadership of Hui Shih (fl. 350-260
B.C.) and Kung-sun Lung (fl. 284-259 B.C.). But the
name of the scholar who did the writing modern scholarship was unable to determine. Still another theory
developed in modern times is that the book indeed
was composed by someone whom we refer to more or
less anonymously as Lao Tzu, or the Old Master, and
carried down orally from generation to generation until it was finally put into written form about the fourth
or third century B.C. A likely candidate for the honor
of having put the work into written form, according
to this viewpoint, is Huan Yu, a Taoist scholar of the
Chi Hsia Academy in the state of Ch'i. Most recent
scholarship in the field has accepted the following con-
clusions: (1) internal evidence of a social and economic nature indicates the work must have been composed in the latter part of the era known as Spring
and Autumn, i.e., about the sixth to the fifth century
B.C.; (2) Lao Tan and Lao Tzu are one and the same
man and the true author of the work, a man some
twenty years senior to Confucius. The labor of scholarship has, we see, come full circle, returning sub-
stantially to the attitude before the eighteenth century when tradition was accepted as truth. Perhaps
the anonymous and mysterious character of the authorship is in keeping with the spirit of *Tao*. Its ori-
gins are as vague and mystic as *Tao* itself. After all,
we are told in the opening sentence of the *Tao Te*

Ching: "The *Tao* that can be told is not the real *Tao* and the name that can be named is not the real name."

Let us forget about the name of the author of the book and concentrate now our attention on the meaning of *Tao.* It has been interpreted and translated variously by different Chinese and Western scholars. However, whether the *Tao* can be translated into words and identified by intellection and rationalization is a question. Even certain Chinese commentators on Taoism have raised the question whether *Tao,* as it is expounded by Lao Tzu, has any verbally expressible meaning, whether it can be defined. P'o Chü-i, of the ninth century, one of the famous Tang poets, comments on this humorously:

Those who speak do not know;
Those who know do not speak.
This is what we were told by Lao Tzu.
Should we believe that he himself
  was the one who knew;
How could it then be that he wrote
  no less than five thousand words.

The question posed by P'o Chü-i and the other critics can be answered by the analogy of Wu-tzu, Fa-yen (?-1104) who says: "I make an embroidery of drakes and let you examine and admire them. As for the golden needle, I cannot pass it on to you." Thus the words of the *Tao Te Ching* comprise the embroidery. They are not the needle itself. But after we admire the art of the embroiderer our minds may open up to the vision of the glittering needle itself.

Let us look at a few examples of Lao Tzu's embroidery:

That which you look at but cannot see
Is called the Invisible.
That which you listen to but cannot hear
Is called the Inaudible.
That which you grasp but cannot hold
Is called the Unfathomable.

None of these three can be inquired after,
Hence they blend into one.
Above no light can make it lighter,
Beneath no darkness can make it darker.

Unceasingly it continues
But it is impossible to be defined.
Again it returns to nothingness.

Thus it is described as the Form of the Formless,
The Image of the Imageless.
Hence it is called the Evasive.

It is met with but no one sees its face;
It is followed but no one sees its back.

To hold to the Tao *of old,*
To deal with the affairs at hand,
In order to understand the primordial beginnings,
That is called the rule of Tao (Ch. XIV).

In this passage Lao Tzŭ identifies *Tao* as the One
which is invisible, inaudible, unfathomable. It is the
same One, past and present; it embraces form and
formless alike, being as well as nonbeing. The One is
therefore a unification of duality and multiplicity. It
is the One without opposite, infinite and unceasing.

In our empirical existence we draw innumerable
distinctions that make for a dualistic view of the universe. There are high and low, great and small, this
and that, black and white, right and wrong, and an infinite number of other dualities. The Taoist asks

whether within these alleged dualities any real distinctions exist. Chuang Tzu puts the problem thus:
"Because a thing is greater than other things we call
it great; then all things in the world are great. Because a thing is smaller than other things we call it
small; and then all things in the world are small." We
all know, as a matter of fact, that size is relative and
subject to change. One stick may be shorter than another and yet longer than a third. Consequently, the
stick embraces the apparently opposed qualities of
longness and shortness.

Proceeding to even more extreme instances of apparent duality, Chuang Tzu says: "There is nothing
in the world greater than the tip of a hair, while the
Mountain Tai is small. Neither is there any life longer
than that of a child cut off in infancy, while P'eng
Tsu [the Methuselah of China, who, according to tradition, lived eight hundred years] died young"
(*Ch. 6*).

Thus we see that each entity possesses qualities
not merely different, diverse, but actually opposite.
Through such an analysis the Taoist attains a synthesis of opposites, or what Hegel calls an "identity-in-
difference." That is to say, *A* is *A*, but at the same
time *A* is not *A*. In the words of Chuang Tzu: "That
which is One is One. That which is not One is also
One" (*Ch. VI*).

Such a synthesis through logical analysis was not
confined to the Taoists but was also found in a school
of logicians who lived at the time of Chuang Tzu.
Hui Shih and Kung-sun Lung are representative of
this school. Among the typical formulations of the
Logicians we find: "There is a point in time when the

head of a flying arrow neither moves nor stops." "One starts out of Yüeh (in South China) today and arrives there yesterday." "Take a stick one foot long and cut it in half every day and you will never come to the end, even after ten thousand years." However, these statements were mere intellectual exercises for the logicians and proceeded no further in the direction of spiritual insight. As we shall see, Taoism was able to go further. A stick in reality is what it is. It cannot be identified by the relative value of either long or short. To realize the self-so-ness of the stick is the essence of *Tao*.

The achievement of Taoism is not merely that of the concept of unity of dualities or the identification of opposites. For the Taoist there is also a unity in multiplicity, a wholeness of parts. In the *Tao Te Ching* Lao Tzu presents a very simple explanation of wholeness:

Thirty spokes joined at the hub.
  From their nonbeing
Comes the function of the wheel.

Shape clay into a vessel.
  From its nonbeing
Comes the function of the vessel (Ch. XI).

The wheel is the wholeness of the spokes and the vessel the wholeness of the clay. In the Taoist sense we may say that the reason the wheel becomes a wheel is that it conforms with the principle of *Tao*, possesses oneness, a wholeness in multiplicity. The same is true of the vessel and the clay.

But even the notion of unity or synthesis of parts into a whole is still far from conveying the deepest meaning of *Tao*. For *Tao* is immanent and yet transcendental. It is indivisible and yet is the source from which all duality and multiplicity proceed. A story in the *Works of Chuang Tzu* illustrates this point:

Tung Kuo Tzu asked Chuang Tzu: "Where is this which you call *Tao?*" "Everywhere," Chuang Tzu replied. "Where specifically?" insisted Tung Kuo Tzu. "It is in the ant," Chuang Tzu answered. "How can it be so low?" "It is in the earthware tiles." "Still worse." "It is in excrement." To this Tung Kuo Tzu did not answer. Chuang Tzu proceeded to explain himself, "Your questions did not go to the heart of *Tao*. You must not ask for the specification of particular things in which *Tao* exists. There is no single thing without *Tao!*" (*Ch. XXII*).

There are three words that can be used to characterize *Tao: chou,* all-pervading; *pein,* all-embracing; and *hsien,* everywhere and all things. This all-pervading and all-embracing *Tao* can be further illustrated in the words of Lao Tzu:

Obtaining the One, Heaven was made clear.
Obtaining the One, Earth was made stable.
Obtaining the One, the Gods were made spiritual.
Obtaining the One, the valleys were made full.
Obtaining the One, all things lived and grew
    (Ch. XXXIX).

The one which is possessed by Heaven, Earth, the gods, and all things is the same one: *Tao*. In other words, *Tao* pervades them and embraces them all. Lao Tzu says:

There was something complete and nebulous
Which existed before the Heaven and Earth,
Silent, invisible,

Unchanging, standing as One,
Unceasing, ever-revolving,
Able to be the Mother of the World.

I do not know its name and call it Tao (Ch. XXV).

Tao, as the mother of the world, all-pervading and
all-embracing, unchanging and unceasing, is conceived
of by Chuang Tzu as *Ta T'ung,* or the grand interfusion. The realm of the grand interfusion is free from
all determinations and contradictions. It is beyond the
reach of all intellectual processes. In this realm there
is neither space nor time; it is infinite. As Chuang Tzu
describes it: "Being is without dwelling place. Continuity is without duration. Being without dwelling
place is space. Continuity without duration is time.
There is birth, there is death, there is issuing forth,
there is entering in. That through which one passes in
and out without seeing its form is the Gate of Heaven.
The Gate of Heaven is nonbeing. All things sprang
from nonbeing" (*Ch. XXIII*). The realm of nonbeing is absolutely free from limitations and distinctions.
In this case nonbeing is the one-without-contrast; that
is, the unity of all things. It is called *Tao,* or The
Great.

When Lao Tzu calls *Tao* the Great, or Mother of
All Things, he means that *Tao* is the primordial source
of every beginning and every end. It is the realm from
which all birth issues forth and to which all death returns. It is all embracing, far reaching, never ceasing,
yet it is the realm of the unknown; so it is called
nonbeing. The realm of nonbeing is the ground of the
great sympathy, or *Tz'u,* as I have mentioned above.
There are two aspects of the manifestation of non-

being: *Ming,*[5] or light, and *P'o,* the uncarved block or original simplicity. They flow mutually to one another. From the ordinary point of view they are separated as two, but from the Taoist point of view they are conceived of as one. They both lead to the great sympathy and are identified with it.

When Chuang Tzu mystically identifies the opposites he speaks of seeing things in the light. He says:

> Affirmation arises from negation, and negation from affirmation. Therefore, the sage disregards all distinctions and takes his point of view from Heaven. The "this" is also "that," and the "that" is also "this." "This" was its right and wrong and "that" also has its right and wrong. Is there really a distinction between "this" and "that"? Is there really no distinction between "this" and "that"? Not to determine "this" and "that" as opposites is the very essence of *Tao.* . . . Affirmation and negation alike blend into the infinite One. Hence it is said there is nothing better than to see things through the Light (*Ch. II*).

To see things through the light is not only to blend opposites into one but it is to enter into the unity of all things.

In this unity everything breaks through the shell of itself and interfuses with every other thing. Each identifies with every other. The one is many and the many is one. In this realm all selves dissolve into one, and all our selves are selves only to the extent that they disappear into all other selves. Each individual merges into every other individual. Here we have entered the realm of nonbeing. The dissolution of self and the interfusion among all individuals, which takes place upon entry into this realm of nonbeing, con-

---

[5] *Ming* is further explained in the chapter on Painting as a symbol in an early script.

stitute the metaphysical structure of sympathy. Chuang Tzu illustrates as follows:

Take for instance a human body consisting of hundred bones, nine external cavities and six internal organs, all of which exist through their complete integration. May I ask which of them I should favor most? Should I not favor them all equally? Or should I favor only one in particular? Are all these organs subordinates of a power apart from themselves? As subordinates cannot govern themselves, do they rather alternate as master and subordinates? Is there not something real that exists through their own integration? (*Ch. II*).

This something real, manifested by the interfusion and interpenetration of multiplicities, is the spirit of the great sympathy, the primary moving force of the universe. Its ground is the realm of nonbeing, and we see it by the light of Heaven, as Taoists call it.

The realm of nonbeing or the ground of the great sympathy has another manifestation, which is called *P'o,* or the uncarved block, manifested in daily living. Lao Tzu says:

Knowing of the Male,
  But staying with the Female,
  One becomes the humble Valley of the World.

Being the Valley of the World

  He never deviates from his real nature
  And thus returns to the innocence of the infant
    (Ch. XXVIII).

The uncarved block, in Chinese *P'o,* has a primary meaning of simple, plain, with no color or markings. The man of *P'o* makes no artificial efforts toward morality and intellectual distinction. His self is merged with all other selves and all other selves are merged in him. But neither he nor others are consciously or purposefully aware of this. "He acts but does not appropriate; accomplishes but does not claim credit." Chuang Tzu describes the man of *P'o:*

They were upright and correct without knowing that to be so was righteousness. They loved one another without knowing that to do so was benevolence. They were sincere without knowing that it was loyalty. They kept their promises without knowing that to do so was to be in good faith. They helped one another without thought of giving or receiving gifts. Thus their actions left no trace and we have no records of their affairs (*Ch. XII*).

What he refers to as "no trace" is an explanation of the character of *P'o.* What is the man of *P'o* like? He says:

In the days of perfect nature men were quiet in their movements and serene in their looks. They lived together with the birds and beasts without distinction of kind. There was no difference between the gentleman and the common man. Being equally without knowledge nothing came between them.

Thus Chuang Tzu describes the achievement of *P'o* and goes on to say again: "It is because they had the quality of the Uncarved Block that they did not lose their original nature" (*Ch. IX*).

This world of the uncarved block is a world of free interfusion among men and among men and all things. Between all multiplicities there existed no boundaries. Man could work with man and share spontaneously together. Each identified with the other and all lived together as one. Man lived an innocent and primitive life, and all conceit and selfishness were put aside. In this uncarved simplicity we see the free movement of the divine. Nature was seen in its marks of spirituality. This we cannot expect in a merely moral and intellectual world, full of distinctions and differentiations. Only in the world of absolutely free identity does the great sympathy exist: the universal force that holds together man and man and all things.

To live in the world of free identity man must transform himself, get rid of his ego-conscious self. Then no problem is set before his intellect, threatening his existence. His self, his intellect, indeed, his whole being is submerged in the world of the unknown, the world of knowledge of no-knowledge. That is why Lao Tzu says:

To reveal Simplicity and to hold the Uncarved Block,
To restrain selfishness and to curtail desires,
To give up learning and to stop worries.
How much difference is there between the politeness
  of wei *and the rudeness of* o? [6]
How much difference is there between goodness
  and badness?
"Where others are afraid I must be afraid, too," is
  extremely ridiculous!
The people are gay as if enjoying a banquet and
  mounting a tower in spring.
I alone, quiet, and unmoved, as a babe unable yet
  to smile, am unattached, depending on nothing.

People all have more than enough;
I alone seem to have nothing left.
So ignorant! My mind must be that of a dolt.
People are bright and shine;
I alone am dark and dull.

[6] *Wei* and *o* are answering inflectional sounds of no specific meaning. *Wei* is a polite response, *o* brusque or rude.

People are clever and distinctive;
I alone am obscure and blunt.
Desolate, as if in the dark,
Quiet as if concentrating on nothing.
People all have purpose and usefulness;
But I alone am ignorant and uncouth.
I am different from all others, but I draw nourishment
from the Mother (Chs. XIX and XX).[7]

What Lao Tzu says is that when one is transformed and at one with all multiplicities he is not self-assertive but disappears into all other selves. So he may be merely ignorant, blunt, and obscure. In short, he is living within the moving forces of the universe and he is himself a part of it. In this connection the Buddhist would say that in the heart of every creature the key to its latent Bodhisattvahood manifests itself as compassion. This compassion, *karuna*, holds all things in manifestation. The universe itself is compassion, *sunyata*, the void. To the Taoist the world of the uncarved block is the manifestation of nonbeing. The great sympathy, or *Tz'u,* is immanent in the uncarved block and flows from nonbeing. The uncarved block and the light, though separate to human sight, are one in reality.

In the chapter on the "Development of Nature" in the *Works of Chuang Tsu* two methods of approach to the state of nonbeing are described, namely *chih,*[8] or

[7] The first two lines of this quotation ordinarily appear in Chapter XIX. However, the original text of *Tao Te Ching* was not divided into chapters. This division into chapters was the work of Ho Shang Kung of the Han Dynasty several hundred years after the time of Lao Tzu. Often these arbitrarily imposed divisions break clear units of thought, as in the instance quoted, where the first two lines are clearly a part of the continuing thought-unit.

[8] The word *chih* when used by the Confucianist means conscious knowledge. But in Chuang Tzu, as herewith indicated, it is used to convey the idea of intuitive knowledge or knowledge of the unknown.

intuitive knowledge, and *t'ien,* quietude, or repose.
According to the tenth-century Taoist named Ssu-ma
Cheng-Chen, the words *chih* and *t'ien* are what the
Buddhists refer to as *ting,* or *dhyana,* and *hui,* or
prajna.

The first approach, through *chih,* or intuitive
knowledge, is a private awareness of one's innermost
being. *Chih* is the key word to understanding *Tao*
and unlocking all the secrets of nonbeing. In other
words, intuitive knowledge is pure self-consciousness
through immediate, direct, primitive penetration instead of by methods that are derivative, inferential, or
rational. In the sphere of intuitive knowledge there is
no separation between the knower and the known;
subject and object are identified. Thus we have the interfusion between the butterfly and Chuang Chou,
and the interpenetration between T'ao Chien, the
poet, and his surroundings. So *chih,* intuitive knowledge, manifested by the interfusion and interpenetration between the universe and all things, is the highest
spiritual power in our possession. It is entirely different from ordinary knowledge.

The usual way of thinking, as Chuang Tzu mentioned, is intellectual dissection and analytical reasoning. The value of such knowledge is relative, limited,
and subject to change. In the process of attaining ordinary knowledge the knower and the known are separate from one another. This knowledge can never
reach to a higher plane. Thus the chapter on the
"Development of Nature" reads in part: "Those who
would develop their own nature by means of ordinary
learning, seeking to restore it to its original condition,
and those who confuse their thoughts by the common

way of thinking, seeking thereby to reach enlightenment, must be pronounced ignorant men." This is true simply because *Tao* cannot be reached by mere intellection. It is only by completely setting aside our rational intellect and excluding conscious supposition that it can be reached.

Therefore the Taoist teaches without words, transmitting through nonexplanation. An allegory of Chuang Tzu goes as follows:

Knowledge journeyed northward . . . and met Do-Nothing-and-Say-Nothing. Of him Knowledge asked: "How must we think in order to come to a knowledge of *Tao*? How is it approached? How do we pursue and attain it?" Do-Nothing-and-Say-Nothing answered not a word because he could not. Knowledge then traveled southward . . . and met All-in-Extremes and put the identical questions to him. "I know," All-in-Extremes answered. And he started to tell him but immediately forgot what it was he was going to say. So Knowledge went to the Yellow Emperor and put his questions to him. The Yellow Emperor replied: "*Tao* may be known by no thoughts, no reflections. It may be approached by resting in nothingness, by following nothing, pursuing nothing. . . . The Sage teaches a doctrine which does not find expression in words" (*Ch. XXII*).

The questions that Knowledge puts in this story cannot be answered because intuitive knowledge cannot be transmitted. It comes of itself, as light at the turning of a switch. In the chapter entitled "The Great Supreme" the process of awakening to enlightenment, or entering into the realm of nonbeing, is compared to that of bursting into sudden laughter. When enlightenment comes, Chuang Tzu says, it is as though one could not contain one's self from breaking into laughter before a story is finished. Te Ching, the great Buddhist of the sixteenth century, comments upon this passage, confirming it as an example of sudden enlightenment. Hsieh Ling-yün, of the fifth century, uses another revealing metaphor. Enlightenment, he says, is like leaping across a chasm or a gulf. Either one succeeds in the leap and attains sudden enlightenment or remains as one was. This is because nonbeing is a higher unity, a oneness. One does not come to enlightenment a little at a time, part today and part tomorrow. Any accomplishment less than this is not oneness.

The theory of sudden enlightenment, indeed, was a significant contribution of Taoism to Buddhist thought in China. In the fourth century the famous Buddhist Tao-sheng started a revolution within Buddhism by taking over this Taoist theory. The movement did much to pave the way for the rise of Ch'an Buddhism in the seventh century. The well-known statement of Tao-sheng attacking traditional Buddhist teaching on enlightenment was phrased like this: "Symbols are to express ideas. When ideas have been understood, symbols should be forgotten. Words are to interpret thoughts. When thoughts have been absorbed, words stop. . . . Only those who can take the fish and forget the net are worthy to seek the truth." [9] In this statement Tao-sheng was almost directly quoting Chuang Tzu:

The fishing net is used to catch fish. Let us take the fish and forget the net. The snare is used to catch hares. Let us take the hare and forget the snare. The word is used to

[9] *Kao-seng Chuan,* or *Biographies of Eminent Buddhist Monks,* chuan 7.

convey ideas. When ideas are apprehended, let us forget the words. How delightful to be able to talk with such a man, who has forgotten the words! (*Ch. XXVI*).

The emancipating effect of the teaching of sudden enlightenment on the development of Buddhism in China was directly attributable to Taoist influence.

It is interesting and significant that the early Buddhist scholars, such as Seng-chao (384-414), Tao sheng (ca. 360-434), Tao yung (died 443?), Seng-jui (373-439), and Hui-kuan (died 453) who assisted the great Indian teacher Kumarajiva in his translations of the Buddhist classics, were also well acquainted with Taoist teachings. From the work of these great Buddhist monks we find the natural outcome a synthesis of Indian Buddhism and Taoism. This eventually led to a distinctively Chinese form of Buddhism, known as *Ch'an* Buddhism or Zen as it is more commonly identified in Japan and in the West.

We find in Buddhist historical records after Tao-sheng's death that his disciple Tao-yu was invited by the Emperor Wen of the former Sung Dynasty (420-479) to preach the theory of sudden enlightenment in the court. Tao-yu challenged and defeated the opposite point of view with a bold and elegant speech. The Emperor slapped the table with delight and declared himself most happy. Later Fa-yu, Fa-pao, Pao-ling, and other monks also preached this notion of sudden enlightenment.

An interesting example of "teaching without words" is often used by the *Ch'an* Buddhists. Long before Hui-neng, early in the sixth century, Fu-hsi was invited by the Emperor Wu of the Liang Dynasty (555-581) to preach the Diamond *Sutra*. As soon as he was seated in his chair in the court he slapped a ruler down upon the table before him. Then he left. This was his teaching. Another day he was discovered in the court wearing a monk's robe, a Taoist hat, and the shoes of a common laborer. The Emperor, seeing him, asked, "Is that a Buddhist costume you are wearing?" Fu-hsi pointed to his Taoist hat. The Emperor asked, "Are you a Taoist?" Fu-hsi pointed to his laborer's shoes. "Are you a common man?" asked the Emperor. Fu-hsi pointed to his fine Buddhist robes. This teaching without words is similar to the Ch'annist teaching through the use of the *koan*. Fu-hsi bore the Taoist courtesy name Hsüan-feng or Mystic Wind, and was certainly influenced by Taoism. It is obvious that long before the sixth Patriarch of *Ch'an* Buddhism the basic philosophy of *Ch'an* Buddhism was preached and practiced openly in the capital of the country.

In this connection we may look at the method of *wen ta* (in Japanese, *mondo*), i.e., the question-and-answer method of teaching enlightenment and entering the realm of nonbeing. Both the *Ch'an* Buddhist and the Taoist mistrust rational intellect as a means toward acquiring a new point of view regarding life and the universe. The aim of *wen ta* or *mondo* is to make the opening wedge in the personality through which enlightenment may come. The *Ch'an* Buddhists are noted for their use of the *wen ta* in connection with apparently trivial incidents in order to open the student's mind into an entirely new way of thinking. Frequently used illustrations are those of the door and the clock. This opening out of the mind through confrontation with the unexpected is like opening a door upon a new world of experience. It is like the gathering of forces within a clock when it comes to strike the hour. The mechanism of the mind seems to have something in common with that of the clock. At a certain moment, in those minds which are prepared for it, the forces of the personality bring themselves together and throw aside the veil that has encircled them, to look out upon a new world about them. The entire make-up of one's life is thereafter altered. The opening, this mental clicking of the mind, is the enlightenment.

We find ample evidence that even the early Taoist feels much the same as the *Ch'an* Buddhist in this respect. Thus we find an interesting example of *mondo* in the dialogue between Lao Tzu and Confucius. Lao Tzu said: "The six classics, as you mentioned, are but the worn-out footprints of the sages of the past. The footprints are made by shoes, but they are not the shoes themselves. . . . Hawks stare at one another, and without moving their eyes their young are produced. There is a male insect which chirps with the wind while the female chirps against it, and thereby their young are produced. There are hermaphroditic animals which produce their own young independently." Confucius reflected upon these remarks for a period of three months and then returned to Lao Tzu and said: "Magpies and their kind hatch out their young from eggs. Fish reproduce their kind by the impregnation of their milt. The wasp gives rise to itself by the process of metamorphosis. When the young brother is born the elder brother cries." Lao Tzu answered: "Good! You have got it! You have grasped the Tao." (*Ch. XIV*). We hasten to add that this story is not a part of the canon of Confucianism, but it does illustrate the method of *wen ta,* or *mondo.*

This *mondo* story suggests another example of *mondo* from the *Ch'an* Buddhist school. The *Ch'an* Master went for a walk with Huang Shan-Ku, the Sung poet. When they walked past a mountain laurel in bloom, the Master asked, "Do you smell it?" The poet answered, "Yes." The Master replied, "There! I have nothing to hide from you!" Both the Taoist and the Ch'annist examples of *mondo* indicate a similar attitude toward enlightenment. We find a Taoist explanation of *mondo* in the works of Chuang Tzu (*Ch. XXII*):

> He who replies to questions about *Tao* does not really understand *Tao.* . . . There is no possible inquiring about *Tao* and there are no answers to questions. Asking questions which cannot be answered is foolish. Answering questions to which there is no answer is to lack inward knowledge. The foolish and those lacking inward knowledge have never observed the workings of the universe and are not aware of the Great Beginning. They cannot cross over the sacred mountain, Kun Lun, and soar away into the Supreme Void or Nonbeing.

The void and the great beginning are one, since when we are in the void, in the one, there is no room for speech. If we speak of the one then the one becomes the object, with ourselves as the subject, and oneness exists no longer in its higher unity. Understanding that we are in the one without speaking of it is the approach to nonbeing through *chih,* intuitive knowledge, or *prajna,* as I have mentioned above.

The other approach is that of *t'ien,* or quietude, or *dhyana,* in the Buddhist term. The approach to nonbeing through quietude is a second basic method described in the works of Lao Tzu and Chuang Tzu and especially developed by the later Taoist priests. The Buddhists often refer to this as gradual attainment. Lao Tzu calls it the losing method. He says: "The student of knowledge learns day by day. The student of Tao loses day by day." Through losing one begins to approach the realm of quietude and enter the realm of nonbeing. And through quietude one strives to return to the deep root of his being and become aware thereby of the deep root of all things. It is the process of seeing and delving into the maternal depths of nature. Lao Tzu says:

Devote yourself to the utmost Void;
Contemplate earnestly in Quiescence.
All things are together in action,
But I look into their nonaction.
For things are continuously moving, restless,
Yet each is proceeding back to its origin.
Proceeding back to the origin means Quiescence.
To be in Quiescence is to see "being-for-itself" [10] (Ch. XVI).

According to the Taoist, when a state of perfect quiescence is achieved all the signs of action of the

[10] *Ming* is often given as fate, destiny, life, and the like. In this context it refers to other than concrete things. Here it is the changeless and formless, which is reached by the process of negation, or cancellation, as Hegel calls it. Since it was impossible to find an identical term in the Western language, I tried to come close to its meaning in the context by using "Being-for-itself," a term given by Hegel. In his *Philosophical Propaedeutics,* translated by William T. Harris, Hegel says, "Inasmuch as the 'state or condition' is canceled through change, change itself also is canceled. Being, consequently, with this process has gone back into itself and excludes otherness from itself. It is FOR ITSELF." Lao Tzu's approach to quiescence, from action to nonaction, is similar to this negative procedure from the changing to the changeless. *Ming,* or being-for-itself, as used here, and *ming,* or light, as used before, are two different characters in Chinese. The English transliteration, according to Wade-Giles, happens to be the same for *ming,* light, and *ming,* being-for-itself; in Chinese these meanings are distinguished by different intonations of the word *ming.*

outside world and one's own will cease and every
trace and mark of limitations and conditions will vanish. No thought will disturb. One becomes aware of a
Heavenly radiance within. It is light in darkness.
When this radiance comes it is said that the golden
flower opens. The blossoming of the golden flower
purifies the heart and the body as well. One gains an
illuminating insight into the pure nature of his own.
Here then is the real self, the inmost being. Chuang
Tzu says:

When one is extremely tranquil then the Heavenly
Light is given forth. He who emits this Heavenly Light
sees his Real Self. He who cultivates his Real Self achieves
the Absolute (*Ch. XXIII*).

To the Taoist the attainment of absolute reality is
to be in the realm of the great infinite, the realm of
nonbeing. To enter the realm of nonbeing is to have
reached the ground of the great sympathy.

One may enter the realm of nonbeing either
through quiescence, *t'ien,* or through intuitive knowledge, *chih.* The former concentrates upon repose, or
what the Buddhists call *dhyana.* The latter stresses
intuition, or *prajna.* The concentration on repose is
often referred to as the method of gradual attainment;
stress on intuition is referred to as sudden enlightenment. Both methods are described in Taoist writings.
But the goal of either method is the entry into the
realm of nonbeing.

Nonbeing manifests itself either as the Heavenly
light or the uncarved block. They are two aspects of
the same thing. In the realm of nonbeing the interfusion and identification of multiplicity takes place as

a manifestation of the great sympathy. Free identification and interfusion in the realm of nonbeing are the functions of the great sympathy. In short, it is the *Tao,* the higher unity of all things.

To summarize: both the uncarved block and the Heavenly light are manifestations of nonbeing; intuitive knowledge and quiescence are the means of entering the realm of nonbeing. The former two can be identified with sympathy and the latter two are the keys by which the mind of man can be opened and through which he can transform his personality and fulfill the demands of the great sympathy.

Identification and interfusion are the basic functions of sympathy according to Taoism, as we have indicated above. Unification of subject and object, the knower and the known, is achieved by immediate, spontaneous interaction. The transformation of man into a butterfly and back again to man, as illustrated in the story of Chuang Tzu, is not a measured or gradated thing. It is a total union through ontological experience, nondifferentiated and nondiscriminated. We learn this from the teachings of Lao Tzu and Chuang Tzu. However, this intuitive and immediate path toward the great sympathy by means of nondifferentiation and nondiscrimination is also clearly shared by the Neo-Confucianists of the School of Mind (since the eleventh century). We have explained that *Jen* is the rational mind of man, which is arrived at through intensive discrimination and distinction. The Neo-Confucianists, who were influenced by both Taoism and Buddhism, conceived of *Jen* as the primordial nature of man, from which fellow-feeling, benevolence, goodness, and love emerge, but none of these is *Jen*. The man of *Jen* by nature loves man, but *Jen* itself is not love. Ch'eng Hao (1032-1085) says that the man of *Jen* is at one with all things and his function is one with that of Heaven and Earth. If we fail to understand this unity then the self and the nonself stand opposed to one another. We must not even strive for unity, for in that case there will be no unity. We must simply cultivate ourselves with the spirit of oneness in our minds. Nothing else is necessary. Such is the heart of spiritual cultivation of sympathy. One should have no "deliberate mind." As Ch'eng Hao put it: "The changelessness of Heaven and Earth is that their mind penetrates all things while they themselves have no mind. The constancy of the sage is that his passion accords with all things, yet he himself has no passion." This explanation of *Jen* as no-mind or no deliberate mind is an approach to the unification of the self and nonself, which is, in fact, the Taoist process of nondifferentiation.

As Ch'eng Hao clearly states, "The *Tao* has no opposite." This idea of the unification of man and the universe can even be found in the *Analects* of Confucius. It is indicated in a story about Confucius and some of his pupils, whom he asked one day to tell him of their ambitions. One said that he would like to be a minister of war, another a minister of finance, still another a ceremonial official in the prince's court. The fourth pupil, Tseng Tien, completely ignored this exchange and quietly strummed his lute. Confucius, when the others had finished, asked him to speak. Tseng Tien answered that he would like to go in the spring to the river bank, where, with his companions, he would bathe in the river, enjoy the breezes, and walk home singing. Whereupon Confucius said: "I approve of Tien."

The Neo-Confucianists comment upon this story that Tseng Tien was eliminating selfish desire and thereby living according to the all-pervading law of Heaven. This was the source of his simplicity and his greatness, both in action and at rest. His mind was so vast that it was at one with Heaven and Earth as in a "single stream" in which all things enjoy themselves. "To rest in the single stream of Heaven and Earth," as the Neo-Confucianists put it, is surely to have attained to the highest realm of spiritual cultivation of sympathy. Here we have interfusion between the minds of the great thinkers of Taoism and Confucianism.

Some of the Western thinkers have also proceeded to the realm of nondifferentiation. We have the example of Meister Eckhart. One of the stories about Meister Eckhart is translated by R. B. Blakney as follows:

A daughter came to the preaching cloister and asked for Meister Eckhart. The doorman asked:

"Whom shall I announce?"

"I don't know," she said.

"Why don't you know?"

"Because I am neither a girl, nor a woman, nor a husband, nor a wife, nor a widow, nor a virgin, nor a master, nor a maid, nor a servant."

The doorman went to Meister Eckhart and said:

"Come out here and see the strangest creature you ever heard of. Let me go with you, and you stick your head out and ask: 'Who wants me?' "

Meister Eckhart did so and she gave him the same reply she had made to the doorman. Then he said:

"My dear child, what you say is right and sensible but explain to me what you mean." She said:

"If I were a girl, I should be still in my first innocence; if I were a woman, I should always be giving birth in my soul to the eternal word; if I were a husband, I should put up a stiff resistance to all evil; if I were a wife, I should keep faith with my dear one, whom I married; if I were a widow, I should be always longing for the one I loved; if I were a virgin, I should be reverently devout; if I were a servant-maid, in humility I should count myself lower than God or any creature; and if I were a man-servant, I should be hard at work, always serving my Lord with my whole heart. But since of all these I am neither one, I am just a something among something, and so I go."

Then Meister Eckhart went in and said to his pupils: "It seems to me that I have just listened to the purest person I have ever known."

To the Chinese Taoist this "purest of persons" would be one who had entered the realm of nonbeing and had appeared as the uncarved block, in all her original simplicity, one who had seen within her the inward light. She was one with the great sympathy and was herself a part of it.

2 Immeasurable potentialities of creativity

○ Probably all of us at one time or another have enjoyed looking at a Chinese painting or have read some Chinese poetry with pleasure. Certain works, I believe, among the productions of the Chinese artists and poets are particularly representative of the spirit of Tao. When we are struck by the utter tranquillity of landscapes by Mi-Fei and Ni Tsan,[1] or moved by the simplicity and purity of poems by T'ao Ch'ien,[2] we come close to experiencing aesthetically what the Taoist hopes to experience spiritually. There is something inherent in these works that leads us to the inexpressible ultimate that man shares with the universe. There is in them a dynamic process that interfuses with a higher grade of reality. They draw us into a spontaneous and even unintentional unity which, as the Taoist sees it, refers back to *Tao* itself, the primordial source of creativity. Only *Tao*, the

[1] Mi-Fei (1051-1107); Ni Tsan (1301-1374).
[2] T'ao Ch'ien (373-427).

mother of all things, is invisible and unfathomable, but it is through her manifestations, nevertheless, that all things are produced. Alfred North Whitehead expressed his central concept thus: "In the philosophy of organism this ultimate is termed 'creativity' and God is its primordial, non-temporal accident." [8] The Taoist, too, says that this ultimate is creativity, that creativity is *Tao*. Since *Tao* is inexpressible, explaining it in terms of the process of creativity is merely resorting to a verbal convenience, or, more precisely, a verbal inconvenience.

Lao Tzu, of course, faced the same difficulty. In one place he turns to the use of numbers in attempting to describe the process of creativity. But his use of numbers is entirely without conventional meaning. In Chapter 42 of the *Tao Te Ching* we read:

From the Tao, the One is created;
From the One, Two;
From the Two, Three;
From the Three, Ten Thousand Things.

The numbers as used here are simply intended to suggest the need for an intuitive awareness of the process of differentiation from nondifferentiation, the realization that the multiple diversities of existence emanate from the unity of the absolute realm of *Tao*. The numbers symbolize what our intellect is unable to explain. The same thing is true of the word process as I use it. I am obliged to resort to such a word in attempting to explain *Tao* intellectually. Actual creativity requires no intellectual explanation in terms of process. It is, rather, a mere intuitive reflection of

[8] Alfred North Whitehead, *Process and Reality*, 1929, p. 11.

things. The following Chinese verse, from the eighth century, may help us to gain some insight into the nature of reflection:

The wild geese fly across the long sky above.
Their image is reflected upon the chilly water below.
The geese do not mean to cast their image on the water;
Nor does the water mean to hold the image of the geese.

This little poem is a metaphor for the idea of reflection as creativity. When the geese fly above the water, they are free of any intention of casting their image upon it, even as the water has no intention of reflecting their flight. But it is at this moment that their beauty is most purely reflected. In this instant of reflection time is space and space is time. They merge at one absolute point, the point from which all beauty, all that is created, arises. Our minds are simply God's mirror, reflecting the "here-now" of creation. Such, according to the Taoist, is the process of creation. But this creative reflection can only be understood through private intuition.

Perhaps I can suggest something more of the nature of this private intuition in the following story, which comes from the work entitled *The Recorded Sayings of the Ancient Worthies*. In the eleventh century Fa Yen, at the age of thirty-five, became a monk and studied the teachings of the Mere Ideation School. Fa Yen, however, was puzzled by the notion that for a bodhisattva entering upon a vision of *Tao, chih* or knowledge (distinction) and *li* or truth (nondistinction) became indifferentiable, and subject and object interfuse as one. Indifferentiability of subject and object, he was told, was symbolized by the man drinking water, who knows, within himself, whether the water is hot or cold. This famous metaphor troubled him for many years. He studied with many teachers but received no enlightenment. But one day, as he reflected upon the saying "The Tathāgata (The Buddha) had secret teachings; but Mahākāsyapa (his disciple) did not keep the secret," he was suddenly enlightened. "Truly so, truly so!" he cried. "Knowledge and truth are indifferentiable. Object and subject are indeed one, even as a man drinking water knows within himself whether it is warm or cold. How true is this statement!" The poem he wrote in reflection upon this moment of enlightenment went like this:

At the foot of the hill a patch of fallow field.
I salute with my hands and ask the old man,
"How many times have you sold the field and bought it
*   back again?"*
"I am fond of the pines and the bamboos enticing the pure
*   breezes."*

This patch of field, sold and bought back again, is nothing other than what one owns in the beginning. What we should do is to turn to what we own within ourselves. Our private intuition is our own. Enlightenment does not come from without. It comes only from within. Buddha's secret is not a secret. It is open to every mind, hidden from none. All one needs is the faith to look deeply enough within one's self, where the light lurks, awaiting our vision.

Enlightenment has been likened to an inward flood:

Last night the spring rains came rushing to the river.
Today the huge ships float like clouds upon the stream.
Vessels that could not stir before
Now travel freely in the middle of the current.

With an awareness of these rising currents within ourselves we may come to an understanding of the creativity of *Tao*. However, the concept of creativity maintained by non-Taoist philosophers is different from this. Let us first examine various non-Taoist concepts of creativity. In the *Works* of Chuang Tzu we read:

How endlessly the heavens turn! And yet the earth remains at rest! Do the sun and moon quarrel as to their positions? Who rules over and orders all these things? By whom are they held together in harmony? Who effortlessly causes and maintains them? Is there, perhaps, some hidden tension which prevents them from being other than as they are? Must the heavenly bodies move as they do, powerless to do otherwise? Look how the clouds drop rain! And how the rain rises again to form the clouds! Who moves them to this abundance? Who effortlessly produces this primary job and stimulates it? The winds rise in the north and blow to the east and west. Others move upward uncertainly. Whose breath moves them? Who effortlessly causes them to blow? What is the cause? (*Ch. XIV*).

To answer these questions Chinese philosophers have put forth many theories. The first is the anthropomorphic vision of a universe directed by a personal God. After study in recent decades of the inscriptions on the ancient oracle bones and the bronzes of the Shang (1766-1122 B.C.) and Chou (1122-255 B.C.) and re-examination of the earliest Chinese classics we have come to realize that the words *Ti* and *T'ien* represent two distinct concepts of God. The former, *Ti*, is a symbol that represents God and ancestor combined. The latter, *T'ien*, Heaven, represents the supreme power of both the personal and later impersonal divine. These two concepts of God paved the way for the later Chinese schools of religion and philosophy.

During the last fifty years one of the important Chinese contributions to the study of ancient culture was the discovery of the oracle bones. Although these bones were originally used for purposes of divination they bear the records of the culture of the Chinese people during the period of 273 years, reveal to us the religious, political, social, and economic activities of the Chinese people more than three thousand years ago. Among these ancient records we find repeated references to religious activities, such as sacrifices and divinations. The words for God, or *Ti,* meant the First Ancestor of the people of Shang. All sorts of problems, such as the conduct of battle, weather and harvest, hunting and fishing, sickness and dreams, and the fate and fortune of the individual, were brought to him. For example, we find the passage, "Within the next two months *Ti,* or God, will not make the rain descend for us." And again, "The King asks that a capital be built and *Ti,* God, has promised that it shall be done." According to Chinese etymologists, the symbol *Ti* was a picture of the calyx and the heart of a flower, from which the generations of the blossoms, fruit, and new plant will develop. Therefore the symbol *Ti* is a clear representation of the earliest ancestor of the people of Shang. The name of this *Ti* was *Kuei,* an ancestor whose name appears repeatedly in both the oracle bones and the earliest classics. He is the Ruler Above, but with over-all power in the world of men. He can grant blessings to men as well as send disaster and punishment. In the latter part of the Shang Dynasty this God was referred to as the Ruler Above, or Supreme Ruler. As to early ancestor worship, in addition to the First Ancestor, *Ti,* or *Kuei,* the people of Shang also made sacrifices to their more recently deceased relatives: grandparents, parents, dead siblings, and others. These ancestors and relatives had influence on the First Ancestor, or *Ti*, because they all lived together high in the Heaven. Thus sometimes, instead of asking blessings directly from the First Ancestor, *Ti*, they directed their requests through closer relatives. An early record reads, "Pray for rain from grandmother *Yi*." Hence the sacrifices to the ancestor (and to God) were one of the chief activities of the people of Shang. Each year eighteen different sacrifices to the ancestors were performed. This concept of God is an anthropomorphic one. It might not be wrong to say that the worship of God in China was originally the extension of ancestor worship and that this was an extension of interpersonal relationships between men. Thus the God of earliest China, before the twelfth century B.C., was an anthropomorphic divine.

The concept of *T'ien*, or Heaven, represents the fundamental religious idea of the Chou Dynasty, the dynasty that followed the period of Shang. The concept of *T'ien* is an illustration of the increasingly expanding idea of God from a personal to an impersonal supreme being. The earliest script form of the word *T'ien* appears on the oracle bones with the meaning, according to the etymologist, simply of sky, or great. When the founder of the Chou dynasty succeeded the Shang rulers, the people, in addition to practicing ancestor worship, inherited from the preceding period the concept of *T'ien*, or Heaven, as representative of the supreme being. This supreme being had sway over all the tribes in the land, unlike *Ti*, the ancestor of the descendants of Shang. Though he was not a creator in the Hebrew sense of God, he was a great and beneficent power who ruled, by reasonable norms, the destinies of men. He guarded the tranquillity and internal order of the mundane world but also caused disasters and meted out punishment to men. In the *Book of Odes* we read: "Illustrious was the House of Chou. And the decrees of Heaven came at their proper seasons. King Wen ascends and descends on the left and right of God. . . . The descendants of the sovereigns of Shang were in number more than hundreds of thousands. But when God gave the command they became subject to Chou." From this passage we see that *T'ien* could be regarded as an anthropomorphic God to whom was attributed more power than to *Ti*, of the Shang Dynasty.

The concept of *T'ien* developed by the founders of Chou as a personal God also contained the notion of God as an impersonal being. The impersonal characteristics of this God are twofold: first, the concept does not depend merely upon the consecrative context, such as sacrifice and divination, as practiced by the people of Shang; the supreme divine can only be revealed to those who cultivate their virtue (or conduct) and form a harmonious social order. In the *Book of Odes* and the *Book of History* there are repeated warnings such as this: "The Heavenly decrees are not reliable." Or, "Cultivate your virtues in order to live up to Heaven. Blessing must be sought by yourself." Secondly, T'ien contained the notion that what is God-given is what we would call human nature. To fulfill the law of our natures is to reveal the heavenly divine. In the *Book of Odes* we read:

"Heaven in producing mankind annexed its laws to every faculty and relationship. Man possessed of this nature should strive to develop his endowment to perfection." Thus, the cultivation of inner tranquillity in man becomes a part of the cosmic order. This notion is very important because it paves the way for many future developments in Chinese philosophy, especially in respect to the idea of creativity.

Besides the idea of *Ti* and *T'ien* related to the idea of creativity, there is the idea of *Ch'i*. *Ch'i* is a word that may be translated in a variety of ways. It means ether, breath, vapor, steam, or matter-energy. The School of *Ch'i* put aside the anthropomorphic God and attempted a materialistic explanation of the universe, in terms of a primal quality of existence, *Ch'i*, which condensed and constituted itself into the various particularities of the cosmos, including man himself.

This pseudo-scientific vein of thought continues, with various refinements, throughout the history of Chinese speculative thought. We find it recurring with new vitality in the great intellectual upsurge that is referred to as Neo-Confucianism and took place in the ninth and tenth centuries. The Sung Neo-Confucianist Chang Tsai (1020-77) speaks for this continuing school of thought, as in his expression of the harmony of the universe of *Ch'i:* "Through the condensation and dispersion of the ether the universe pushes forward along a hundred different roads; its principle for so doing is orderly and real."

"The Great Void cannot but consist of ether; this ether cannot but condense to form all things; and these things cannot but become dispersed so as to form once more the Great Void. The perpetuation of these movements in a cycle is inevitably thus."

This simple materialistic approach of Chang Tsai applies to all life:

Animals derive their being from Heaven. Their progression through the successive stages of growth and decline depends upon the intaking and the exhaling of the breath. The being of plants comes from the earth. Their progression through the successive stages of growth and decline depends upon the rising and falling movements of *yin* and *yang*. When a creature is born the ether day by day enters into it and increases. When this creature passes its maturity the ether gradually withdraws and becomes dispersed. Its entering, while it is increasing, is of the spirit; its going out, when it returns to its source, is of the ghost.

We must not be deceived by references to spirit and heaven and such concepts. The entire orientation of the School of *Ch'i* is purely materialistic.

Up to the period of Chang Tsai, to whom I have referred above, creation was considered in a purely material sense, as a matter of the origination of primal substance, i.e., in terms of *Ch'i*, ether. Later philosophers were not satisfied with this view of creation. Chen Yi and Chu Hsi, in the eleventh and twelfth centuries, felt that the materialism of *Ch'i* must have some ultimate principle behind it that determined its creative character. This principle they referred to as *Li*.

Chu Hsi says: "The creation of man depends simply upon the union of the principle with the ether. Heavenly principle, or *T'ien Li*, is surely vast and inexhaustible. All men's capacity to speak, move, think, and act, is entirely derived from the ether; and yet within this ether principle inheres." *Li* is formal cause, *Ch'i* material cause. In the metaphysical world, beyond substance, is *Li,* or principle. All things, including man, must at the moment of their creation receive *Li* in order to establish their peculiar nature.

The world of principle, however, is vast and pure, but empty. It is in itself shapeless, formless—though it creates all form. It is without will or power. Only in coordination with the material world of *Ch'i* does it manifest itself in the sensory world. Principle is eternal, transcending space and time. When a house is built it is constructed of substantial items: brick, wood, mortar. But there must be a plan whereby these substances are organized into a meaningful whole. The material is *Ch'i,* the plan *Li.* When the house has been constructed according to plan it manifests *Li* in its concrete form.

Principle exists before its objectification. Thus before the cart, or the ship, exists, there already exist the principles of their being. Invention, thus, is merely the discovery of existing principle. The created actuality must conform to the principle. It becomes thus the physical embodiment of the eternal idea. For every potential actual existent there must be an eternal concept in the world of principle. The world of principle itself, therefore, is all-complete and all-perfect.

The Taoist concept of creativity is of self-realization, which requires no outward instrumentality to effect its inward processes. *Tao* is the inner reality of all things. It depends upon neither external God, nor concrete substance, nor abstract principle, as various other Chinese schools of philosophy maintain. Such would imply a limitation upon *Tao,* and *Tao* is limitless. Chuang Tzu illustrates the idea for us thus:

> . . . those who rely upon the arc, the line, compasses, and the square to make correct forms injure the natural construction of things. Those who use cords to bind and glue to piece together interfere with the natural character of things. . . . There is an ultimate reality in things. Things in their ultimate reality are curved without the help of arcs, straight without lines, round without compasses, and rectangular without right angles. . . . In this manner all things create themselves from their own inward reflection and none can tell how they come to do so (*Ch. VIII*).

When inner reflection takes place it fulfills the process of manifesting ultimate reality. This process is direct, immediate, and spontaneous. The curve simply reflects its curve, the line its straightness. The flower blooms in the spring and the Moon at night shines upon the lake. It is as the wild geese that I spoke of at the beginning of this chapter. They cast their images upon the water completely without intention. Such spontaneous reflection is the creativity of *Tao.* But always *Tao* itself remains invisible and unfathomable. What we grasp, what we see, is simply its manifestation through reflection. Lao Tzu says: "*Tao* never acts, yet through it nothing is undone. . . . All things create themselves" (*Ch. XXXVII*).

Whitehead explains this concept of self-creativity in Western terms: "Creativity is without a character of its own. . . . It is the ultimate notion of the highest generality at the base of actuality. It cannot be characterized because all characters are more special than itself. But creativity is always found under conditions and described as conditioned." [4]

This is what the Taoist would refer to as self-creativity. We can only see creativity in its manifestations, only as conditioned. "*Tao* never acts, yet through it nothing is undone." "Changes take place by themselves, without movement; things reveal themselves, without display." The *Ch'an* Buddhist puts it more vividly: "As long as it remains in itself, all is quiet. The mountain remains a mountain, towering up to the sky. The river flows along as a river, singing its way down to the ocean. But as soon as a tiny speck of cloud appears in the blue, it in no time spreads out enveloping the whole universe, even vomiting thunders and lightnings." [5] At this point, fully charged with the creative *elan vital,* human intellectuality often loses sight of it, and moves on bewildered, vexed, full of fearful thoughts. To be free from the confusion of external conditions, to be rid of the perplexities of life, to be fully charged with primordial creativity, is to attain *Tao.*

In the previous chapter I have discussed *Tao* as sympathy. *Tao* is, to be sure, the great mother, the infinite, free from conditions of time and space. From this point of view it is the one-without-contrast, non-being, the higher unity. This is to see *Tao* as the unification of infinite possibility and potentiality. It is the unity of multiplicities. Here we have the ontological basis for the fulfillment of the great sympathy.

But to understand creativity as a process we must

---

[4] Whitehead, *op. cit.,* p. 47.
[5] Daisets T. Suzuki, *Eranos-Jahrbuch* 1954, Vol. XXIII, p. 280.

approach *Tao* from the reverse direction. We must see *Tao* as having penetrated into infinite multiplicities and into the manifold diversities of existence. Sympathy moves from all to one, creativity moves from one to all. Without sympathy there is no ground of potentiality to support creativity. Without creativity there is no means of actuality to reveal sympathy. Sympathy and creativity move together hand in hand. In unity there is the infinite interfusion of diversities but in each diversity we find the total potentiality of unity.

Kuo Hsiang, the Neo-Taoist of the fourth century, illustrates this concept thus: "A man is born but six feet tall. . . . However insignificant his body may be it takes a whole universe to support it." This idea of unity within multiplicity is also elucidated by the Chinese Buddhist: "The lion with all his hairs, taken together, is at the same time found within a single hair." The lion with all his hairs indicates unity and the single hair indicates a particularity in multiplicity. To see the unity within multiplicity is to see infinite potentiality manifested in each particularity. This vision is a Taoist contribution to the understanding of creativity.

Let us consider this basic groundwork of creativity —unity within multiplicity—in more detail. According to the Taoists it is only in the world as manifested that we are confronted with polarities and multiplicities. In the absolute realm these opposites and diversities are completely interfused and identified. Chuang Tzu says: "If we see things from the point of view of their differences, then even our inner organs are as far apart as the states of Ch'u and Yüeh.

But if we see things from the point of view of their identity, then all things are one" (*Ch. II*). To see things relatively is to recognize them in their diversities; but in an absolute sense, diversities are reconciled into unity. The former represent the all, the latter represent the one.

Chuang Tzu gives us an illustration of this idea in the centipede. From the relative point of view the insect, of course, does have its hundred or so different legs. But from the higher point of view there is a unification of multiplicity. The coordinated movement of all the legs is a manifestation of unity. From this unity we see the centipede as a whole. All penetrates into one. And the movement of all the legs is an interpenetration of the one into the all. This mutual interpenetration of the one and the all was also illustrated by the famous Buddhist theory of "the realm of Indra's net" [6] and was further ingeniously expounded by a Chinese Buddhist, Fa-tsang, whom we have mentioned before. In the *Sung Compilation of Biographies of Eminent Buddhist Monks* we read that Fa-tsang arranged ten mirrors, one at each of the eight points of the compass, and placed the other two mirrors above and below, all facing one another. In the center he put a small figure of Buddha and illuminated it so that the reflection was cast into each mirror. Each mirror as well, of course, reflected the image of every other mirror, each multiplying and redoubling each other's images endlessly. The one mirror takes in the nine

[6] This net is a metaphor used to illustrate the unobstructed complete interfusion of all particularities in universality. Each pearl in every single loop represents particularity, and the net itself represents universality. Each pearl reflects every other pearl, and in turn, every other pearl reflects this one. Thus in the realm of the net there is endless reflection and interfusion of particularities.

other mirrors, and all nine others at the same time take in one. In other words, one is in all, and all is in one. As soon as one absorbs all, one penetrates into all. As soon as all absorbs one, all penetrate into one. The conclusion is that not only all is in all, and one is in one, but all is one and one is all. In this way the inner reality of multiplicity is perfectly and completely interfused and identified. In Chuang Tsu's expression: "All things and I are one." He further explains that "Only those who understand that interfusion is identification can follow non-action and remain to be ignorant. To be ignorant is the action which means interfusion" (*Ch. II*). This idea of interfusion is better interpreted by Hua Yen's expression *shih shih wu ai,* or "unobstructed complete interfusion," which means that each individual event in the world of events mutually and simultaneously enters, draws in, embraces, and is being embraced unimpededly. It suggests the infinitely complicated interplay among all particularities in the world of events.

When all particularities move into one, each particularity embraces all other particularities, together entering into the one. This doubling and redoubling process ontologically represents the great sympathy. When one enters into all, one embraces all particularities and enters into each. Such a process represents the great creativity, which is supported by all the vitality of sympathy. It is illustrated by the Buddhist in the saying, "Many hairs have an infinitude of lions and this infinitude of lions of these many hairs is further contained within each single hair." When creativity manifests itself the potentialities of all the infinitude of particularities enter into each particularity. Lao Tzu says: "Obtaining the One, Heaven was made clear. Obtaining the One, Earth was made stable. Obtaining the One, the Gods were made spiritual. Obtaining the One, the valley was made full. Obtaining the One, all things lived and grew" (*Ch. XXXIX*). The one is the source of creativity. From the great one are created all the glories of the world.

In the process of creativity each particularity retains the potentialities of the unity. The human eye fails to see this unity and detects only its manifestations in multiplicity. "All things," the Taoist says, "are created by themselves." But in each instance of creativity there is the infinite potentiality of unity. "Heaven and Earth is nothing but a finger, and ten thousand things is nothing but a horse," Chuang Tzu says. So too, feels the Ch'annist who, lifting his finger, perceives the universe to move with it. The lifting of a finger is the slightest of gestures, but when it is viewed from the vantage point of the absolute moment it generates the power of the divine and blossoms into creative vitality.

To see unity in multiplicity is one approach to the understanding of creativity. There is another approach immediately and inseparately related to it. Unity can never remain static. It is both static and dynamic at once. In its static aspect we see it as changeless. In movement we see it as changes. Besides understanding the unity within multiplicity we must attempt to see the changeless within the ever-changing. Until we have done this we cannot comprehend the power of the great creativity. When unity remains within itself it is changeless. When it reflects itself it creates, and changes manifest themselves. To understand the complete process of creation we have to understand, as well, the concept of the changeless within the ever-changing.

The Logicians of the time of Chuang Tzu said: "There is a point in time when the head of a flying arrow neither moves nor stops." The commentator explains this saying: when during one instant of time an object is at two points, it is in motion. When in the interval of two instances of time an object stays at one point, it means that it does not move, and if, in one instant of time, an object stays at one point, it means that it neither moves nor not moves. This ingenious interpretation is, of course, a merely logical one. The Taoist would say that the flying arrow represents the changeless within the ever-changing. In a relative sense, which is conditioned by space and time, the arrow moves from point to point, and from one second to another. Thus we detect its movement. But, from the absolute point of view, which is free from temporal and spatial limitations, there is no apparent movement at all. Thus we see its changelessness. The arrow moves all the time, but at the same time it does not move at all. To quote the Buddhists: "Though things move, they are forever motionless; though things are motionless, they do not cease moving."

Lao Tzu says the *Tao* created the one. From the one arises two and eventually the ten thousand things. These numbers indicate change, but within them runs the thread of the changeless, the *Tao* that is motionless. In manifestations we see change. In the absolute we see the changeless. In this connection I recall the famous remark of Seng Chao, a philosophical monk of the fourth century: "When Heaven and

Earth turn upside down this does not mean that they are not motionless. When the breakers dash heavenward there is no reason to believe that they move."

Chuang Tzu says: "The existence of things is like a galloping horse. With every motion it changes. Every second it is transformed" (*Ch. XVII*). And in another place he says: "Ten thousand things are inherent in the germ, but they undergo changes from one form to another. Their beginning and end are like a circle, no part of which is the same as any other part" (*Ch. XXVII*). The germ is the symbol of the changeless. The forms of the ten thousand things indicate change. Without the germ, the changeless, there is no manifestation. Our understanding of this must come intuitively, not logically. Lao Tzu teaches us this intuitive approach, as mentioned before. In Chapter XVI we read:

All things are together in action, but I look into their non-action, for all things are continuously moving, restless, yet each is proceeding back to its origin. Proceeding back to the origin means quiescence. Quiescence means being-for-itself. Being-for-itself means the ever-changing changeless. To understand the ever-changing changeless is to be enlightened.

When we are enlightened we understand the ever-changing changeless. We see changes as an accumulation of units, or monads, or an indefinite process of repeating and adding things, but the changeless is an invisible, indefinable, complete oneness. There is no differentiation of parts and whole within the changeless. Chuang Tzu explains: "The Sages contemplate ten thousand years and conceive them as a pure complete oneness" (*Ch. II*). The spiritual man, that is, does not rigidly attach himself to particularities, but interfuses with the whole, the oneness of the ten thousand years. He makes himself one with every change. Thus he integrates himself and wanders with solidarity. He is a synthesizer of variations. All distinctions become meaningful. Each change appears in the new situation full of meaning. Changes, however, mean differentiation and determination. But the changeless, as pure complete oneness, should be free from determination and differentiation. Through self-contemplation the changeless is always trying to preserve its self-identity, and yet it subjects itself to infinite possibility and potentiality. When the changeless remains in itself and with itself it is continuum, quiescence, oneness. When it subjects itself to change it creates. Change is not something imposed upon it, I must make clear, but a product of self-generation. From the changeless we come to the reservoir of creativity. In the manifestations of the changeless we see its reflection. This reflection is derived from the boundlessness of space and the endlessness of time. The boundlessness of space and the endlessness of time refer to the ultimate reality of all things, unity within multiplicity. From the changeless to the ever-changing we see creativity in the process of transition; from unity to multiplicity we see creativity in the process of concrescence. Both concrescence and transition are in the grip of what Whitehead has called the "creative advance into novelty." In fact, concrescence is in transition and transition is in concrescence. In the absolute realm of creativity they are identified.

Neo-Confucianists explain the process of creativity in the universe with full realization that concrescence and transition are one. This idea can be illustrated by the *T'ai-chi Tu,* or *The Chart of The Supreme Ultimate,* of Chou Tun-yi, whose character was highly esteemed by his followers as a man with his feelings "free and unforced as the fresh breeze and the bright moonlight in an unclouded sky."

In the explanation of the Chart Chou says:

That which is the Ultimateless, is also the Supreme Ultimate.[7] The Supreme Ultimate moves and creates *yang.* When the movement reaches its utmost it returns to quiescence. Quiescence creates *yin.* When the quiescence reaches its utmost it returns to movement. Movement and quiescence alternate and thus mutually originate one another. When *yin* and *yang* function distinctively two forces are clearly revealed. By unification *yin* and *yang* transform themselves into fire, water, wood, metal, and earth . . . (in fact) the five elements are the same as yin and yang; yin and yang are the same as the Supreme Ultimate. The Supreme Ultimate primarily is the Ultimateless. When the five elements are produced each possesses its specific nature. The reality of the Ultimateless, the essences of the two forces and the five ele-

[7] The meaning of the Chinese original text, *Wu chi erh T'ai chi,* is extremely ambiguous. It can be interpreted in either of two ways: (1) *wu chi,* which yet itself is also *T'ai chi,* means that the Ultimateless is simultaneously the supreme ultimate; (2) from *wu chi,* and then *T'ai chi,* which means that from the ultimateless is produced the supreme ultimate. The controversial issue provoked a serious war between two leading Neo-Confucianists, Chu Hsi and Lu Hsiang-shan. The former scholar took the first interpretation, the latter the second. Chu Hsi maintained that primordial nature does not at all contain nothing, and that the ultimateless is the same as the supreme ultimate. His intention was to protect the philosophical system of Chou Tun-yi from charges of being influenced by Taoism or Buddhism. Since Lu attacked the *Diagram,* which was influenced by Lao-Tzu's thought, his interpretation was that from the Ultimateless is produced the supreme ultimate. As a matter of fact, Chou Tun-yi was deeply influenced by Taoism. And in Chapter 40 of the *Tao Te Ching* we do read: "The ten thousand things are produced by Being: Being is produced by Nonbeing." In this chapter the second point of view is maintained. However, the author does not agree with Lu's criticisms of Lao Tzu and Chou Tun-yi.

ments, all unite wondrously so that consolidation ensues. The *ch'ien* principle becomes maleness and the *k'un* principle becomes femaleness. By interfusion the two forces create ten thousand things. Through their producing and reproducing ten thousand things transform themselves and reach no limitation.

In this process from the ultimateless to the ultimate, from movement to quiescence, from *yin* and *yang* to five elements and from the *ch'ien* and *k'un* principles to all things we see transition: the ever-changing in the changeless. From the union of the two forces, the five elements, the *ch'ien* and *k'un* principles, and the essence of all forms and all elements we see the process of concrescence, unity within multiplicity. Both the changeless and unity are the same in the realm that Chou called the "ultimateless."

From the Taoist point of view the ultimateless-ness of the universe is duplicated in man. The man of enlightenment achieves the ultimateless. When he contemplates he sees ten thousand things as pure complete one. He intuits the changeless within the ever-changing and identifies with both. He sees multiplicities and diversities in their essential unity. Heaven and earth and all things are as one. He who comprehends both processes, that of the unity within multiplicity and the changeless within the ever-changing, and becomes an integral part of both processes, has attained enlightenment. Being enlightened, he is free from the entanglements of time and from the attachment to things. Yet he identifies with all that is temporal and spacial, shares in its common essence. "I receive nourishment from the Great Mother," as Lao Tzu says. This interfusion and identification between self and nonself is the source of all potentialities, all possibilities, and moves in the realm of absolute reality. Thereby his reflection is filled with the creative spirit that animates all things. Such effort cannot be artificial. It is a pure, true immediate reflection of ultimate reality. We call it the process of creativity. When man is in this creative process he is truly egoless: as egoless as the Moon and the stars.

One of the great contributions of Chinese philosophy is the theory that man perfects himself through the cultivation of egoless selfhood. The teachings of both Taoists and Buddhists rest on this theory. Even the Confucianist school goes along with this notion, more in ethical than metaphysical terms, to be sure, but with implications that go beyond ethical considerations. Confucius himself, for example, was described as having succeeded in freeing himself from four great hindrances: preconceptions, predeterminations, obduracy, and egoism.[8] The Neo-Confucianists took this hint and developed it in great detail, expounding a theory that aimed at the transformation of the ego to the self. This vein of thinking, indeed, runs throughout Chinese philosophy.

We are none of us without our higher qualities of selfhood. Many of us, however, decline to accept the pull of these higher spiritual aspirations. They are buried deeply beneath willfulness, desires, pride, and artificial intellection. The aim of the Chinese philosophical teachings is to open out what is hidden within. It is directed toward answering the call of our higher inward qualities.

There are two main approaches toward releasing

[8] Confucian *Analects,* Book IX, Ch. 4.

these higher qualities of selfhood and penetrating to the source of creativity. Advocates of these two schools constantly quarrel as to their respective merits. These two approaches are those of discrimination and differentiation as opposed to nondiscrimination and nondifferentiation. In China these two points of view are represented by the Confucianist and the Taoist schools of thought.

Let us first examine the Confucianist approach. A premise that always lies behind Confucianist thinking is that conscious knowledge and its tools are the key to the Heavenly order. The Confucianist thinker strives intellectually to seek out the rational principle of things, which is called *li*. For the Confucianist, everything in the universe has its own principle, but all the ten thousand principles exist at one and the same time in the universe, innately within the mind of man. Through the exhaustive study of the innumerable external things mankind gains his way to an understanding of the nature of the mind. When man reaches the utmost point in his exhaustive studies he is led to complete enlightenment. Then all the multitude of things, "external and internal," "fine or coarse," are visible clearly to him by the light of his own nature. The Confucianist goal is *ch'eng,* which has been translated as sincerity, perfection, realness. In *The Doctrine of the Mean, ch'eng* is referred to as the way of Heaven, the beginning and end of things. The attainment of *ch'eng* is the way of man. He who possesses *ch'eng* is he who, without an effort, hits what is right. The process of the attainment of *ch'eng* is best outlined in the *I Ching* thus: "Through exhaustive study of principles one fulfills one's own nature. The utmost fulfillment of one's own nature reaches to the Heavenly Order."

Through such an effort of analysis and differentiation man is, the Confucianist says, able to develop his conscious knowledge to the point of fulfilling his nature. Because the Confucianist conceives the universe as a conscious entity, man must attempt to emulate the pattern of the universe and, by identifying with its rational meaning, become one with it. This attitude is expounded in detail by the Confucian School of Principle, which was notably represented by Chu Hsi (1130-1200). Here is the theory in Chu Hsi's words:

No human intelligence is completely devoid of conscious knowledge. And nothing in the world is without its reason, its principle. But because man has not completely exhausted his study of the principle of things his understanding is yet incomplete. The first lesson of the Great Learning is instruction to the student to proceed from those principles which he understands to the further understanding of those principles which yet lie beyond him. Only by lengthy exertions will he come eventually to a complete understanding. But then, with complete understanding of the multitude of things . . . will the mind be opened to enlightenment.[9]

Chu Hsi, thus, advocates the analysis of things as the route toward enlightenment. The effort works through conscious knowledge. This attitude has been argued against by Chu Hsi's contemporaries and by modern Chinese thinkers. It is, of course, diametrically opposed by the Taoists, who, in quite contrary fashion, have always maintained the need for reducing conscious knowledge. They rather cultivated intuitive

[9] *The Great Learning*, Ch. 5.

knowledge or *Chih* in order to attain enlightenment. This is the knowledge of no-knowledge, or genuine knowledge, as Chuang Tzu calls it.

A contemporary of Confucius named Wang T'ai was famous in his time in the state of Lu, where he shared honors with Confucius himself as a great master. Wang T'ai was marked by a physical deformity, having lost one of his legs. Yet his students were as numerous as those of Confucius. Chuang Tzu explains that Wang T'ai's mind was so stable that even if the Heaven and Earth fell on him he would not move. He knows the meaning of changes and does not grasp at externalities, but sees their inner reality. He sees things from the point of view of identity, in their unity, not in their imperfections.[10] Wang T'ai, Chuang Tzu says, possesses "genuine knowledge" and thereby transforms his ego into self. The process of this attainment is described thus: "By self-cultivation through genuine knowledge (i.e., knowledge of no-knowledge) man obtains his mind (the mind of harmony). Through this mind (of harmony) he obtains the absolute mind."[11]

A famous commentator, Chang T'ai-yen, equates the word mind in this passage to the Buddhist concept of *ālaya,* the eighth consciousness, which is the storage house of the unconsciousness. Absolute mind is identified by Chang T'ai-yen as *agada,* or pure consciousness. Absolute mind, or pure consciousness, is completely without content, spotless, undefiled. It is often referred to as the Heavenly light. The Taoist process of transformation of the ego to the self is, thus, through

[10] *The Works of Chuang Tzu,* Ch. V.
[11] *Ibid.*

knowledge of no-knowledge or nondifferentiation, to reach the storage house of the unconscious. From *ālaya* emanates pure consciousness, or Heavenly light.

According to the Taoists the analysis of things succeeds only in separating object analyzed and subject analyzer. When the analyzer and the analyzed are two, the ego persists in its function of differentiating and prevents the emergence of the great self; whereas nondifferentiation, or knowledge of no-knowledge, seeks to break down the boundaries between analyzer as subject and analyzed as object. Interpenetration of the two gives rise to the mind of harmony. This mind of harmony, as we have said, may be compared to ālaya, the reservoir of life. From this unconscious storage house, pure consciousness or light emanates. Thus enlightenment takes place and the self is transformed. The Taoist sees the ego as a hard core, which can be broken only by the energy of the unconscious, which penetrates it, turns it inside out. Only thus can the great self be released. This derivation of light from the deep layers of the unconscious is not an analytic process. Logical understanding, indeed, is foreign to it.

Let us return for a moment to the Confucianist approach to self-transformation and the attainment of creativity. The Confucianist approach was essentially intellectual, but even among the early Confucianists there was a contrary theory that stressed what was referred to as *chih chü,* or "confronting the crooked and the bent." This is the concept of experiencing the dark shadow, or the dark aspect. In the *Doctrine of the Mean,* i.e., as early as the fourth century B.C., there had already been conceived the notion that, in addition to fulfilling one's rational nature, one should look inward to confront the "crooked and the bent." We read, "In the crooked and the bent there is *ch'eng*, realness. Being real, it becomes apparent. Being apparent, it leads to pure consciousness. Being purely conscious it becomes enlightenment." The early Chinese Confucianists, in other words, though they stressed the fulfillment of one's rational nature through the rational analysis of things, they, too, fully realized the importance of the confrontation of the dark aspect. Through rational analysis alone, without the confrontation of the dark aspect, one cannot attain enlightenment and self-transformation. Although Chu Hsi maintains achievement of enlightenment through analytical approach, he does not neglect entirely the depth of unconsciousness that must be confronted through non-differentiation. As he says in his poem:

We study the Changes (I Ching) after the lines have been put together.
Why should we not set our minds on that which was before any line was drawn?

The Neo-Confucianist School of Mind, founded by Lu Hsiang-shan (1139-1193) opposed the analysis of principle and the increase of rational knowledge. The School of Mind advocated the reducing of knowledge, the "letting go" of all rational knowledge. When that is done, Lu says, "All that is left is my mind and I as a man." The mind to which he refers is original mind. The man to whom he refers is the enlightened man. Lu describes himself as enlightened: "I lift up my head and grasp at the Great Dipper. I turn my body round and am in the company of the North Star. With my head erect I look beyond the Heavens. There is no

such man as I." Lu does not deny his existence, but
rather identifies himself with Heaven. He, in fact, attained enlightenment through the method of nondifferentiation. The story goes that one day he was
reading an ancient writing in which he encountered
the following passage: "The four points of the compass and all that is above and below make up what is
called *yü*. The past, the present, and the future make
up what is called *Chou*." Upon reading these words
Lu suddenly experienced the sense of identification
with the universe at the absolute point of "here-now."
"All the affairs of the universe come within the range
of my duty," he declared. "My duties include all the
affairs of the universe." And again he said: "The universe is my mind. My mind is the universe." [12] Lu's
method may be called comprehending the fundamental, i.e., reducing one's knowledge, and having confi-
dence in one's self. As he once said: "If in learning a
man comprehends what is fundamental the *Six Classics*
are only footnotes." [13] If one has faith in one's self one
will be suddenly enlightened through self-realization.
There is no need to waste time and energy on endless analysis.

I have gone through the biographies of the leaders
of both schools—the School of Principle and the
School of Mind—and I find the experience of enlightenment only among those who belonged to the School
of Mind. The following two stories provide more evidence that enlightenment must come through immediate intuitive nondifferentiation and nondiscrimination.

[12] *Complete Works of Lu Hsiang-shan*, Vol. XXXIII.
[13] *Ibid.*, Vol. XXXIV.

The first story comes from the biography of Yang Chien (1140-1226):

About the year 1169 Yang Chien was appointed assistant prefect in Fu-yang. He had often heard Lu Hsiang-shan speak of original mind. One evening he asked, in a measured manner, of Lu Hsiang-shang, "What is meant by the expression, the 'original mind'?" It happened that earlier the same day Yang had heard in court the case of a fan vendor who had brought a suit at law. So now Lu replied loudly, "In the case of the fan vendor you were able to see who was right and who was wrong and thereby to pronounce your judgment. What is this if not knowledge that comes from the original mind?" On hearing this, Yang suddenly experienced the enlightenment of his own mind.

Here we have a case of sudden enlightenment experienced by a Confucianist. Although in the story Yang seems to appeal to the intellect—the difference between right and wrong in pronouncing judgment—what actually penetrates Yang is the immediate intuitive approach to the root of his thoughts, whence the differentiation of right and wrong is derived. It is not the differentiation that causes Yang's enlightenment. It is the direct spontaneous response from his innermost being in one total flash. In Yang's own writings we find the following passage: "When I inquired about the meaning of original mind Master Lu explained by way of reply the rights and wrongs involved in that day's case of the fan vendor. Then I suddenly experienced the enlightenment of my mind, and that this mind has no beginning or end and penetrates everywhere." In Yang's work entitled *Of Self and Changes,* we have his further explanation: "What is

Heaven is a symbol within my own nature; what is Earth is a form within my own nature. . . . Undifferentially all permeate one another. By observing a single line in the hexagram the meaning of the self becomes suddenly apparent." Here Yang explains why he has had his sudden enlightenment. From the single line he derives the unification of multiplicities, the unification of man and all things. This single line is oneness, or nondifferentiation.

Another story of the experiencing of sudden enlightenment by a Neo-Confucianist is recorded in the biography of Wang Yang-ming (1472-1529). The relevant passage reads thus:

In the third year of the Cheng-te Period (1508) when the master was thirty-seven years old, in the third month of the spring, Master Wang was exiled to Lung-tsang District in the mountainous Kuei Chou Province. It was a rough district, inhabited by snakes, scorpions, wild animals, and even more savage people, who could scarcely understand Chinese. Wang's only acquaintances to whom he could talk were his fellow exiles. Here, however, he came to realize that all the honor, fame, and all the insults and slights that he had been exposed to were really of no consequence. . . . He had to chop wood, carry water, cook, and do every manual task. He occupied himself in writing poetry to be sung to the local folk tunes and to consoling the ill among his followers. He thought deeply during this period, wondering often what the Sage would do under similar circumstances. Suddenly in the middle of the night he was enlightened. He unconsciously cried out and jumped from his bed. His followers were astonished. But from then on Wang realized that what the Sage teaches us exists already, self-sufficient, within ourselves. What he formerly sought for through analytic principles was incorrect.

When we analyze this instance of sudden enlightenment we see that through Wang's struggle with hard-
ship the realities of life penetrated his innermost being. No differentiation any longer existed in his mind
as to the diversities of things: fame and failure, gain
and loss, self and nonself. In this extreme situation he
came to sudden enlightenment. From his own account
his former method of seeking the principles of things
through analysis was wrong. We can safely say that his
sudden enlightenment was through immediate, direct
self-realization. From the illustrations I have given it
is apparent that enlightenment and transformation of
ego to self must begin with nondifferentiation.

We find the approach of nondifferentiation outlined
as early as the times of the *I Ching:* "Changes mean no
thought and no anxiety. Silently it is immovable. When
it moves it penetrates, thereupon, to all things in the
universe." Thus the author who was influenced by
Taoism, too, believes that our nature reaches its highest development only when we cultivate ourselves spiritually to the point where we achieve union with all
things. To describe this process Cheng Hao (1032-
1085) says: "By exhaustive study of principle and development of nature to the utmost one attains to the
Heavenly order. All three are attained at the same
time. Basically there is no sequence in this attainment.
The exhaustive study of principle cannot be considered
as something belonging to knowledge." This principle
is that of nondifferentiation. Man and the universe are
one.

Finally, let us look at the frame of mind of the man
who has this genuine knowledge of no-knowledge. I

will let Lieh Tzu, a contemporary of Chuang Tzu, speak for himself.

After nine years' study I can set my mind completely free, let my words come forth completely unbound as I speak. I do not know whether right and wrong, gain and loss, are mine or others. I am not aware that the old Master Shang Szu is my teacher and that Pai-kao is my friend. My self, both within and without, has been transformed. Everything about me is identified. My eye becomes my ear, my ear becomes my nose, my nose my mouth. My mind is highly integrated and my body dissolves. My bone and my flesh melt away. I cannot tell by what my body is supported or what my feet walk upon. I am blowing away, east and west, as a dry leaf torn from a tree. I cannot even make out whether the wind is riding on me or I am riding on the wind.[14]

When he is not conscious of whether he is riding on the wind or the wind is riding on him, Lieh Tzu is purely in reflection, not conditioned by any externality. His mind is free as the smooth surface of the lake against which the image of the wild geese is spontaneously reflected. This pure reflection gives us no intervening moment for consideration or analysis by the tools of the intellect. It is a flash of lightning, a spark struck from a stone. It needs no passage of time. It is immediate, without deliberation. It does not admit of hypothesis and conclusion. It is an echo from the valley of the struck gong. It is the passing of a shadow, the play of light upon the lake, the wind moving among the leaves. In short, it is nonaction which immediately gives way to action. Or we may say it is absolute nonaction, which is not in contrast to action. In this stage

[14] *Works of Lieh-Tzu,* Ch. 2.

one is no longer attached to either action or nonaction, one transcends both as they are ordinarily conceived. The mind attains illumination and is absolutely free. It is a bright mirror free for its creative function. Those who can reflect freely and purely as nature reflects the passing moods of the day are those who have achieved the light of *Tao* as the great creativity.

There is the story of how Liang-chieh (807-869), who lived in the ninth century, was once fording a river with an older friend. Liang-chieh asked him on this occasion, "How should we ford a river?" He answered, "Do not wet our feet." To ford the river without wetting one's feet is the way of doing things without being attached to them. Or in Lao Tzu's words: "You understand *Tao* as if you did not understand it." To be free from the entanglements both of the external and the internal is what the Taoist calls "the wonder of *Tao*," the primordial source of creativity.

3 Peace as identification of reality and appearance

The word peace in Chinese is *ho p'ing* which, more precisely, means harmony and tranquillity. In a relative sense it is the opposite of discord. Harmony and discord through their polar relationship successively and ceaselessly interact to create the history of mankind and the advancement of the world. The highest sense of peace is what we might call, in the words of Whitehead, "a deep underlying harmony," which is inherent in both man and the universe. It is the ground of all harmonies, from which emanates the all-expanding energy that constantly creates a new universe. Without it nothing that is real can be achieved. It is invisible and unfathomable, beyond the realm of discursive thinking. It can only be experienced as a profound inward feeling, an immediate reflection of deep metaphysical insight, which is unverbalized and yet momentous in its action. We cannot define and point to it, but we may echo the tone of the inner realm of those who have achieved this sense of peace when we read or chant their poetic expressions. Let us try to communicate the inner voice of some of the great poets. First we come to listen to Li P'o (701-762):

You ask me why should I stay in this blue mountain.
I smile but do not answer. O, my mind is at ease!
Peach blossoms and flowing streams pass away without
*   trace.*
How different from the mundane world!

The poet's sense of delight cannot be expressed in words. It is the deep underlying harmony of the nature of all things, in which there is no record of blossoming or fading peach flowers, and no lament upon the symbolic meaning of the never-returning stream, such as Confucius once made while standing at the bank of a river: "It passes on like this, never ceasing, day or night!" The immediate reflection of the highest sense of peace is identified neither as intellectual understanding nor as sentimental emotion, but rather as an instantaneous insight into reality, which makes us feel infinitely blessed while experiencing it. It is our absolute mind that identifies all differentiations, and is unconditioned by any dichotomies or opposites. The poem of Li P'o, however, could not serve as a *kung an* (or *koan* in Japanese), according to *Ch'an* doctrine because, on the one hand, the poet smiles and gives us no answer; on the other hand, he tells us how completely his mind is at ease, that the world in which he lives is delightfully different from the mundane world. His mind still holds something enchanting and is not yet entirely free from it. The following poem of Wang Wei (699-759) will serve as an example of how indescribable is the absolute mind.

Of late I deeply devote myself to quiescence.
Nothing in the world concerns my mind.

. . .

. . .

The breeze from the pine woods blows my sash;
The mountain moon shines upon my harp.
You ask me to explain the reason of failure or success.
The fisherman's song goes deep into the river.

To involve one's self in the disputatious dichotomies
of failure and success means to be trapped in endless
complexity. Instead, when our poet gives his answer
he only mentions something else, irrelevant to the
question put to him. Although he does not say that
his mind is at ease, and that the world in which he
dwells is different from the mundane world, we can
feel that his unfolding inner realm is untainted and
free from any conditioning. His answer without answer
is like a bamboo shadow sweeping the stone steps without stirring up the dust. Yet it is this irrelevant answer that reveals the depth of underlying harmony
and opens the minds of others.

Turning from poetry to another art, we can perhaps
find this deep underlying harmony also in painting.
And indeed, here we see a concrete and direct comprehension of the power of the highest sense of peace.
When an artist introduces certain fineness of form and
color into the welter of incoherent fragments, welding
them thereby into an existential unity, such process of
refinement gives us an apprehension of perceptual values and feelings. However, our aesthetic pleasure is
derived from a mere spatio-temporal pattern of sensa.
The harmony achieved from "the pattern sensa" is a
"qualitative harmony," the harmony of the lower

senses conditioned by objective situations. This relative harmony is constantly subject to change and disorder outside the pattern or form imposed by the artist. On the other hand, in Ch'annist or Taoist painting, the straight line of a bamboo or the gnarled lines of a pine tree do not merely convey a visual impression or arouse physical sensation, but their simplicity and directness, their completeness and movement flow out from the picture and penetrate into our inner being. When we stand before the paintings of Liang Chiai, Ma Yuan, Mu ch'i, or Mi Fei, there is no impetus for an analysis of conceptual components, but our attention is drawn inward and we feel something in us unfolding the mystery of our hearts. By what means is it that the artist opens up the secrets of our hearts? There is no particular beauty in the picture, but there is wholeness, freedom of motion, and freedom of expression, overflowing and removing the mutually excluding opposition between the painting and ourselves. Thus we throw our whole being into the beauty and move along with it. To exemplify this feeling we have Laurence Binyon's personal experience to speak to us:

I recall a little painting of uncertain date but inspired by a poem of Wang Wei the eighth-century poet-painter; the subject is just a sparse wood of stunted trees on a flat foreland: misty water and still sky. Nothing of what to the average mind is beautiful; yet in this foreland scene there was something strangely moving, just because the painter had absorbed the solitude of trees and water into himself. He had painted it internally, so-to-speak, not as something alien and seen from the outside. . . . With Chinese, space often becomes the protagonist in the design. It is not final peace, but itself an activity flowing out from the picture into our minds, and drawing us into a rarer atmosphere. It is tranquilizing, but even more so, it is exhilarating.[1]

The activity of the landscape in the picture reaches the mind of the observer and immediately draws him into a rarer atmosphere. It may be somewhat the same kind of atmosphere from which the painter absorbed the solitude of the trees, water, and sky: the atmosphere that he reproduced from within. Thus, also the painter may be said to have liberated himself by entering into this rarer atmosphere. So it is true, too, of the genuine admirer of the painting.

What is this atmosphere that moves from objects painted to the painter himself? And thence from the painting to the observer? This is the movement of the deep underlying harmony that interfuses and interpenetrates between man and man, between men and things. It emerges with the immediate reflection from the absolute reality of our selves. There is a Ch'annist saying, "Willows are green and flowers red." But at the same time it is said: "Flowers are red yet not red; willows are green and yet not green." The first affirmation is to indicate the facts of our experience accepted as "suchness." It is the immediate reflection. The second statement involves both affirmation and negation, but they are not contradictory to one another. It helps us, rather, to enter the realm of absolute reality, because in this realm there is no need for the process of rational analysis or discursive thinking. What is affirmation is negation and what is negation is affirmation. This is true even on so elementary a level as the flow-

[1] Laurence Binyon, *The Spirit of Man in Asian Art*, p. 98.

ers and the willows. Both are red and not red, both are green and not green. It is by such simple steps that we enter into and unlock the nature of boundless infinitude, thus losing our ego-selves. It is in this direction that lies the cultivation of spiritual intuition and the achievement of absolute freedom.

What the painter produced is the absolute reality of objects as he felt them through the free play of intuition. So in the painting, the subject is expressed from within—sparse woods, still sky, misty water—nothing intrinsically beautiful to the average mind. Yet the absolute reality that derives from this simple expression of space through the medium of the painter's "inner brush" becomes something that moves with absolute directness and force into the mind of the observer. Binyon says: "What he (the painter) put into his work comes out from it and flows over into our minds; and we recognize something which cannot be called intellectual only, sensuous only, or emotional only; it is wholeness of spirit which goes out, free and unafraid, into wholeness of universe." [2] This wholeness of universe is what he means when he refers to a rarer atmosphere. It is what Whitehead refers to as the underlying harmony. And the movement from object painted to painter, from the painting to the observer, is, to turn to Buddhist phraseology, *Yuan yung wu ai*, or "complete unobstructed interpenetration" of things, a manifestation of nature's mysterious capacity of interfusion and interpenetration. It is the same atmosphere that our poets Li P'o and Wang Wei find inexpressible in words.

[2] *Ibid.*, p. 99.

In the history of Chinese painting we have numerous illustrations that reveal this sense of spiritual intuition, a "wholeness of spirit" that moves freely and fearlessly into a "wholeness of universe" in a way that Laurence Binyon has described for us. Perhaps one more illustration will help us. It is, perhaps, the most radical story of its kind.

During the eighth century Wu Tao-tzu (d. 792) completed his last masterpiece for the royal court. It was a landscape painted on a wall of the court. Wu Tao-tzu worked patiently on it in solitude and kept the work draped until it was completed and the Emperor arrived for its unveiling. Wu Tao-tzu drew aside the coverings and the Emperor gazed at the vast and awesome scene and its magnificent detail: woods, mountains, limitless expanses of sky, speckled with clouds and birds, and even men in the hills. "Look," said the artist pointing, "here dwells a spirit in a mountain cave." He clapped his hands and the gate of the cave immediately flew open. The artist stepped in, turned, and said, "The inside is even more beautiful. It is beyond words. Let me lead the way!" But before the Emperor could follow or even bring himself to speak, the gate, the artist, the painting and all faded away. Before him remained only the blank wall with no trace of any brush marks.

This charming story is intended to reveal directly to us that within the outward appearances of all beauty there lies the rarer atmosphere, or the "unity of background," as Binyon calls it elsewhere, which serves as the ultimate reality of all appearances. It is through this ultimate reality that our minds are opened to see our own wholeness of spirit, and enter into the wholeness of the universe, the deep underlying harmony of all things.

According to the Taoists, our daily life gains its significance by being rooted in a deep underlying harmony, or ultimate reality. So long as we deviate from the world of reality, we can never reach true peace. What we may and often do achieve is a kind of pseudoharmony, which we often confuse with reality. It is only when the absolute reality impresses itself upon our daily life in a lively manner—that is, through our activities—that our daily life gains its real value. Only in this way will we be able to order our lives with an inward harmony and a higher sense of peace. In the second chapter of Chuang-tzu, we have a metaphor illustrating the inner harmony between absolute reality and outward activities:

Once the Penumbra asked the Umbra: "Previously you were walking and now you have stopped; previously you were sitting and now you have stood up. Why is it that you lack stability of intention?" The Umbra replied: "It is because what I do is in accordance with the movements of something else. . . . My accordance with the movements of something else is like the accordance of the snake with its scales and the accordance of the cicada with its wings. How can I know why I do one thing and not the other?"

The actions of the Umbra, in movement or at rest, sitting down or standing up, are the various appearances of something else, which is the ultimate reality. Appearance must belong to reality—indeed, it is an expression of reality. Appearance must, we see then, be one with reality.

This is exactly what Lao Tzu said in the first chapter of the *Tao Te Ching*:

Oftentimes without intention I see the wonder of Tao.
Oftentimes with intention I see its manifestations.
Both of these are the same in origin;
They are distinguished by names after their emergence.
Their identification is called mystery.
From mystery to further mystery there is an entrance to
* all wonders.*

To explain this mystery of the identification of appearance and reality, we may find it helpful to turn to some of the basic concepts of the Hua yen School of Chinese Buddhism, which was mentioned briefly in the chapter on creativity.

First, let us look at the two basic ideas, *Shih* and *Li*. *Shih* means event, or form. In the ordinary sense it is an event that refers to a happening. But in the *Book of Changes* we read, "That which is solved by changes is *Shih*" (Hsi T'su). This definition of *Shih* is similar to the concept of event as expounded by Whitehead. "A molecule," Whitehead says, "is an historical route of actual occasions, and such a route is an event." [3] This is to say that an event is really its actuality in the process of motion. Event is more than its static condition. The ever-changing event is what is called *Shih*. It is particularity in action.

Li, in its ordinary sense, is reason or principle, but by the Hua yen School it is often used in the ontological sense, as meaning the absolute or reality, and eventually it means void or nonbeing. It always stands contrasted to *Shih* and, therefore, is universality in action, all-embracing and all-pervading. Hsuang Shih-li, a well-known Chinese philosopher, in his *Treatise on New Mere Ideation*, expounds *Li* as the essence of

[3] Alfred N. Whitehead, *Process and Reality*, p. 124.

reality, which consists of both void and silence. Void does not mean nothingness in the sense that something once was and now is not. It is the ontological foundation from which event or form manifests itself. Therefore, *Li* and *Shih* are not separate existences, but they are completely interfused. Thus *Li* is *Shih,* and *Shih* is *Li.* Ch'eng kuan (738?-839?) illustrates this by a comparison to wave and water. He says that there is no wave that is not water; and there is no water that could not be a wave. Likewise, the mind of the sage is the mind of the common man. Buddha and sentient being are mutually absorbed. Hua yen scholars also maintain that "*Li* does not dissolve in *Shih,* for what is pure (Absolute Reality) is ever mixed (manifested appearance). (Similarly) *Shih* comprises *Li* in its entirety, for what is mixed is ever pure. *Li* and *Shih* exist freely by themselves, yet there is no impediment between what is pure and what is mixed." [4] The theory that *Li* and *Shih,* or reality and appearance, are essentially one is also clearly phrased by Francis Herbert Bradley: "The Reality is nothing at all apart from appearance. . . . Reality appears in its appearances, and they are its revelation; and otherwise they also could be nothing whatever." [5] Thus two elements, *Li* and *Shih,* or reality and appearance, though they are both necessary aspects of the one being, cannot, in truth, be separated entities. Nor can they be scrutinized or removed from one another without obscuring their essential nature. In fact, the world of reality is none other than the world of sense and intellect: the world of sense and intellect is none other than that of

[4] *Hua-yen Yi-hai Pai-men,* p. 630.
[5] F. H. Bradley, *Appearance and Reality,* p. 489.

reality. There is one complete world. To illustrate the absolute oneness between *Shih* and *Li* we may refer to the parable of the Golden Lion.

In the seventh century when Fa-tsang, the founder of the Hua yen School, was lecturing at the royal court, he was faced with the difficulty of expounding the theory of the unobstructed interpenetration of *Shih* and *Li,* or the identification of appearance and reality. Fatsang pointed to a golden lion in the court and delivered his famous parable. Gold symbolizes reality, and the lion, he said, symbolizes appearance. ˙Reality is formless by itself but assumes any form that circumstances give it. Similarly, gold has no "nature of its own" but is shaped into the form of a lion as its appearance. On the other hand, the lion is merely a form or an appearance, which has no reality of its own—it is entirely gold.

When gold absorbs the lion completely, the lion has no existence as a separate entity. The existence of the lion is wholly dependent upon the existence of gold. Without the gold there would be no lion. That is to say, without reality there can be no existence of appearance. On the other hand, the lion represents the appearance of gold; without the form of the lion there is no expression of gold. Appearance reveals the existence of reality. The gold and the lion harmoniously co-exist; they are merged together, but this by no means impedes either from being itself. Each is perfect and sufficient to itself and of itself. The gold and the lion remain distinct in themselves. When one sees the lion, one sees it as a lion; the lion is evident, the gold is neglected. When one sees the gold, the gold is evident and the lion is obscured from sight. At times both can be seen; at other times neither is seen. When the mutual conditioning of gold and lion is in perfect harmony, the dichotomy of *Li* and *Shih* is gone. Words become useless and the mind is absolutely at rest. Reality is appearance, appearance is reality. The gold is the lion, the lion is gold. When appearance and reality are perfectly identified, no words can express this identification: our mind is simply and abruptly enlightened. This is what Chuang Tzu means when he speaks of "Heavenly identity." "Heavenly identity" is what Lao Tzu calls the "mystery," the same origin of reality and appearance: what Whitehead calls the deep underlying harmony.

It is this idea of "mystery" that Chinese painters and poets use to such rich advantage in their works. The "sparse woods, still sky and misty water" which, Binyon says so perfectly, identify the rarer atmosphere of the painting, has its parallel in the story of the Golden Lion. The atmospheric reality of the painting penetrates perfectly into the form of tree, of sky and of water, just as the gold is completely absorbed by the lion. The tree, the sky, and the water are the rarer atmosphere of the painting; the rarer atmosphere is the tree, the sky, and the water. In short, appearance and reality are completely identified and nothing hinders their interfusion. Though the forms of tree and sky and water cannot be said to be beautiful in the ordinary sense, as Binyon explained it, it is through their wholeness of spirit that we are led to see the harmony of harmonies, the origin of all beauties.

We have been trying to see what the Taoist means when he speaks of the underlying harmony of reality. This task is necessarily a difficult one, especially when we begin with the realization that it is impossible to put it into words, and that it can best be approached by indirect suggestion. In order to understand this better, I think we might turn briefly to Bradley's speculations on the nature of reality. Of course Bradley's approach, in its major aspect, is a rational and analytic one. It obviously would be absurd to identify British idealism with Chinese Taoism. However, Bradley has approached the question in a way that I find strikingly important for us as we proceed in a way so markedly different.

Bradley, after a great deal of hair-splitting analysis on the nature of truth and thought, realizes, even as the Taoists do, the limitations of thought in coming to grips with reality. In his work, *Appearance and Reality,* in replying to his critics, he clearly maintains: "Reality is above thought and above every partial aspect of being, but includes them all. Each of these completes itself by uniting with the rest, and so make the perfection of the whole. And this whole is experience, for anything other than experience is meaningless." [6] Bradley attempts to reach reality by intellectual analysis, but he discovers that there is limitation of attainment inherent in discursive and rational thought. According to him, thought is a necessary step toward the attainment of reality, but reality itself is above thought and above every partial aspect of being. It is rather, he asserts, by experience or, as he says elsewhere, a higher immediacy by which we grasp the nature of reality. This higher immediacy is the wholeness of experience, which, as he says, must be immediate, like feeling, but, not like feeling, immediately at the level below dis-

[6] F. H. Bradley, *Appearance and Reality,* p. 493.

tinction and relation. In the process of approaching reality we inevitably reach a stage which is beyond thought, where mere intellection becomes helpless, and we can only intuitively experience it. Therefore, at the conclusion of his work, *Appearance and Reality*, he announces openly that reality is spiritual. He says: "Reality is one Experience, self-pervading and superior to mere relations. Its character is the opposite of the fabled extreme which is barely mechanical, and it is, in the end, the sole perfect realization of spirit. We may fairly close this work then by insisting that Reality is spiritual." What is this realization of spirituality of which Bradley speaks? Is it not the process of the awakening of a new consciousness? In Chinese philosophy, the new consciousness is not conceived of as new at all. It is the self-consciousness to be realized to the fullest depths; that is, consciousness itself turning inward into itself. In Zen's expression, it is the seeing of one's own "original face" before one is born. Therefore, the realization of spirituality as "one experience" or awakening of a new consciousness is simply the consciousness coming to its own unconsciousness. In the Taoist expression the former is *T'ai Chi* or ultimate, the latter, *Wu Chi,* or the ultimateless. The perfect realization of spirituality as one experience is expressed by Lao Tzu as a "Return to the Ultimateless."

In this connection I must point out that we are neither to identify Bradley's system of reality and thought with the system of Chinese Taoism nor are we to neglect the self-contradictions in his discussion of reality, as pointed out by his critics. But what I want to say is that beyond the limitation of intellectual analysis, Bradley proceeds from thought to thoughtless, "beyond thought," and from intellection to high immediacy or "one experience."

It requires a great mental effort on our part to view all things, in their dissimilarities and relations, as one thought. This thought is the thought of the thoughtless, which clearly contains no boundary of differentiations and distinctions. It is spiritual, "a sole perfect realization of spirit." When the mind reverses its usual course and, instead of dividing itself externally, goes back once more to its inner unity, it has begun to move to a state that we may call "one-thought-viewing." In fact, our habitual mind is overdevoted to thought and analysis. Our thinking process tends to dissect reality in order to better understand it. Even though these dissections be reassembled into a whole, they can never regain their original inner unity. They are no longer parts of the same oneness.

It is only when oneness—"one thought"—is reached that we have enlightenment. This is our inner awareness of ultimate reality, not knowledge intellectually acquired. Intellection is necessarily dualistic because it always implies subject and object. But when we break loose from the bounds of relative knowledge and are able to view the ten thousand things in one thought, then there is no longer a separation between knower and known. In this connection, Bradley says, too, that immediate experience opens the one road to the solution of ultimate problems. It is knowing and being in one, a direct awareness, which is nonrelational, and which is neither explainable nor describable. What then is this nonrelational and inexpressible oneness? It is the origin of all beauties, all truth, and all advancement. This viewing of all qualities in one

thought, which finally cuts off the hopelessly entan-
gling logical mesh by merging all difference and likeness into the absolute oneness, has been stressed in the
Tao Te Ching. In chapter 39 we read:

In the ancient times there were those who achieved the
   One.
Achieving the One, Heaven was made clear,
Achieving the One, Earth was made stable,
Achieving the One, God was made spiritual,
Achieving the One, the valleys were made full,
Achieving the One, all things lived and grew. . . .
All of them became so through the One.

Without purity, the Heavens would shake,
Without stability, the Earth would quake,
Without spirituality, God would crumble,
Without fulfillment, the valleys would crack,
Without the power of growth all things would perish.

Oneness, as Lao Tzu saw it, was the primordial
source of all things, the mother of the world. It is the
harmony of harmonies, the highest sense of peace,
which is invisible and unfathomable. Lao Tzu described it further in these words:

The countenance of the Great Achievement
   is simply a manifestation of Tao.
That which is called Tao
   is indistinct and ineffable.
Ineffable and indistinct,
   Yet therein are forms.
Indistinct and ineffable,
   Yet therein are objects.
Deep-seated and unseen
   Therein are essences.
The essence is quite real,
Therein is the vivid truth.
From ancient times until the present,
   that which is called Tao *has never ceased to exist.*

Through it we see manifestations of all the admirables.
How do we understand the way in which
   the admirables become admirable?
It is through Tao (Ch. XXI).

Tao is the reality from which all admirables are manifested. Latent in it are forms, objects, essences, but itself is formless and imageless. We can understand it only through immediate intuition, not through intellection. When we refer to the explanation of peace by Whitehead, we can better understand this ancient idea. Whitehead says:

There is the deep underlying Harmony of Nature, as it were a fluid, flexible support; and on its surface the ripples of social efforts, harmonizing and clashing in their aims at ways of satisfaction. . . . Amid the passing of so much beauty, so much heroism, so much daring. Peace is then the intuition of permanence.

Whitehead says further:

The essence of Peace is that the individual whose strength of experience is founded upon this ultimate intuition thereby is extending the influence of the source of all order.[7]

Now we see both the Eastern and the Western philosophers lead us to believe that the essential truth that peace demands is the conformation of appearance to reality. There is the absolute reality from which all multiplicities spring. We are further convinced by Bradley that reality is above thought that cannot be reached by rational analysis, but only by immediate intuition. This is also advocated by Whitehead. To an-

[7] Alfred N. Whitehead, *Adventures of Ideas*, p. 369.

swer this we have the Taoist philosophy of sudden enlightenment, and its further development by the *Ch'an*
Buddhists.

According to Lao Tzu and Chuang Tzu, enlightenment is the uncovering of hitherto unknown powers of
the mind. To them the opening of the mind is like
bursting into sudden laughter, as mentioned before.
There are unknown recesses in our minds, which lie
beyond the threshold of the conceptually constructive
consciousness. Sudden enlightenment is like breaking
through the conceptual structure of consciousness, setting free the powers imprisoned in the depth of the unconscious.

As long as man fails to set free his potentialities hidden in this innermost region, he is divided against himself. Instead of grasping the key to the secrets of creation, his mind is hopelessly buried in the superficiality
of things. Not until he has liberated himself from im-
prisoning intellectual artificiality is he equipped to
view the universe and man with ontological intuition.
In my chapter, "Invisible Ground of Sympathy" I
briefly told a story from the classics concerning a meeting of Confucius and Lao Tzu. I would like now to go
into it more fully: When Confucius, not yet having
achieved *Tao,* went south to see Lao Tzu, he was
asked: "I hear that you are the wise man from the
north. Have you also received the *Tao?*" "Not yet,"
Confucius replied. The other went on, "How have you
sought it?" Confucius said: "I sought it in rituals and
rules, and after five years I had not yet achieved it."—
"And how then did you seek it?" Confucius said: "I
sought it in the principles of *yin-yang,* but after twelve
years I had not yet found it." Lao Tzu then explained:

"The reason why the *Tao* cannot be transmitted is none other than this: if there is not a presiding center within, it will not remain there." Lao Tzu continued: "It is fortunate that you have not met with a ruler fit to rule the world. The *Six Classics* which you mentioned are but the worn-out footprints of the sages of the past. The footprints were made by the shoes, but they are not the shoes themselves. Hawks stare at one another and without moving their eyes their young are conceived. There is a male insect which chirps with the wind while the female chirps against it, and their young are thereby produced. There are hermaphroditic animals which produce their own young independently." It was said that Confucius reflected upon these remarks for a period of three months and then returned to Lao Tzu and said: "Magpies and their kind hatch out their young from eggs. Fish reproduce their kind by the impregnation of their own milt. The wasp gives rise to itself by the process of metamorphosis. When the younger brother is born, the elder brother cries." Lao Tzu was so pleased with his answer that he explained: "It is well indeed! You have grasped the *Tao*." [8]

This dialogue, which was used by Lao Tzu to open the mind of the zealous learner from the North, and by which the latter passed his examination, seems illogical and nonsensical to us. Yet it was by means of this that the mind of Confucius, according to Chuang Tzu, was unfolded to the full bloom of enlightenment. Confucius' former methods of learning—the *Six Classics*, rituals and rules of the past, the differentiations of *yin-yang* principles—were built upon a logical basis and

[8] Chuang-Tzu, Chapter XIV.

approachable through rationality, but they were of no assistance to him in his spiritual life. Lao Tzu was thoroughly aware of what Confucius failed to see; that he was hopelessly trapped in the realm of relativity and superficiality and was not free to dive into the recesses of the mind where no logical analysis can ever reach. Therefore, in their interview, the master wanted to close down all possible avenues to rationalization in the mind of Confucius. An iron wall was needed to block his every intellectual effort. Lao Tzu's nonsensical statements concerning the reproduction of hawks, insects, and animals served to build that iron wall. Thus the march of thoughts from Confucius' former habitual consciousness had been suddenly excluded. Troubled and agitated, he wanted to break through the wall. Throwing his entire being into the deepest resources of his nature had unexpectedly opened up an unknown region in his mind; it was the birth of a new consciousness, which was truly beyond mere intellection. After three months of self-cultivation, Confucius returned to Lao Tzu and made the same kind of unconventional statement as had his master Lao Tzu: "When the younger brother is born, the elder brother cries."

This direct opening of one's innermost being takes place in the midst of illogical and uncommon expressions. Such direct way of awakening the new consciousness is far beyond the approach of intellectual analysis. The secret cannot be found in intellectual abstraction and metaphysical subtlety; the truth of *Tao* really lies in the concrete realities of our daily activities.

This idea of naturalness was further applied to human relations by Neo-Confucianists. As Wang Yang-ming of the fifteenth century said: "According to Confucianism, between father and son we find love; between ruler and subordinates, righteousness, while with husband and wife, each pursues his own duty. How can we say that there is an attachment through a relationship as natural as that between father and son, ruler and subordinate, husband and wife?" This conception of naturalness was particularly stressed by Taoist philosophers.

We may turn to a simple and amusing story to learn a basic lesson. A student of Zen approached his Master one morning with the question, "What is the essence of Zen?" In turn, the Master asked, "Have you finished your breakfast?" "Yes," was the reply. "Then," answered the Master, "go and wash your dishes." The Master was not being flippant or indifferent. He was simply saying that it is naturalness that leads to enlightenment. As Kuo Hsiang, the Neo-Taoist philosopher of the third century, once said: "The universe has all things as its content, and all things must take 'self-so-ness' as their norm. What is spontaneously so, and not made to be so, is naturalness." In the *Tao Te Ching* we have: "Man follows Earth, Earth follows Heaven, Heaven follows Tzu-Jan, or Self-so-ness." Through Self-so-ness man achieves *Tao* and is enlightened. Self-so-ness is the key to the highest sense of peace.

I should like to illustrate this once more by the following analogy in the second chapter of the works of Chuang Tzu. It is a dialogue between two Taoists, Tzu Ch'i and Tzu Yu, who are discussing the great harmony of the music of Heaven.

"The breath of the Great Earth," says Tzu Ch'i, "is

called the wind. At times it is merely inactive. But when it is in action, the ten thousand crevices of the earth resound and roll with a mighty roar. Have you not heard it in the outburst of a gale? In the projecting bluff of the mountain forest, the hollows of the huge trees are like nostrils, mouths, and ears, others like beam sockets, goblets, mortars, or pools and puddles. The wind whirls through them, like swirling torrents of whizzing arrows bellowing, shouting, trilling, wailing, moaning, roaring, purling. . . . Finally the tempest is over and all crevices became quiet and still. . . ."

"Now," asked Tzu Yu, "since you said that the music of Earth comes from the sounds made by the hollows and crevices, and that the music of Man comes from bamboo pipes and flutes, I venture to ask of what consists the music of Heaven." "The Heavenly music," Tzu Ch'i answered, "blows through ten thousand apertures and through each in a different way. Each of them is self-assertive. What need have they for any agency to excite them?"

What, then, is the music of Heaven? It is nothing more than the music of Earth and the music of man asserting themselves. In the relative sense, we see the difference between the music of Earth and the music of man, and the difference between their separate apertures. But in the highest sense there is a unity, or harmony, between the music of Earth and the music of man. When each aperture, whether of Earth or of man, spontaneously fulfills its natural capacity, the great harmony is attained. This is the music of Heaven. The music of Heaven then is the self-assertion of each aperture of the music of Earth and each instrument of the music of man. Self-assertion is identified with diversity, yet within all diversities there is unity. Unity is invisible, and diversity is tangible. Yet without diversities there is no expression of unity. Without the invisible unity there is no possibility of the great harmony. Whitehead says: "The Great Harmony is the Harmony of enduring individualities connected in the unity of background. It is for this reason that the notion of freedom haunts the higher civilizations. For freedom in any one of its many senses is the claim for vigorous self-assertion." [9] What Whitehead calls "the vigorous self-assertion of freedom" is what Chuang Tzu implied when he speaks of the music of Earth and the music of man in its reflection of the "unified background" of the music of Heaven.

We return once again to Chuang Tzu's analogy, that the ultimate reality is the "music of Heaven." This parable of Chuang Tzu has not been well understood. An interpretative commentary by the great seventeenth-century scholar Yao-Nai, however, provides an enlightening vision: "To a man who has achieved the Self of Non-Self, all music, whether from pipes or flutes or the wind through nature's apertures, is Heavenly music. But to the man who has not achieved this Non-Self, these sounds are still heard as the Music of Man and the Music of Earth."

There is a story from the annals of *Ch'an* Buddhism that bears on this point. It is about a young monk who spent many years wondering about a saying that a famous monk had made. This monk was reputed to have said, "Existence and non-existence are a wisteria vine which twines around a tree." The young student

[9] Whitehead, *op. cit.*, p. 362.

finally made an enormous journey to see this monk and verify the saying. He finally arrived and found the old Master building an earthen wall. Breathless, he asked if he had truly made the remark about the nature of existence and nonexistence. The old monk readily admitted that he had and questioned the young man as to why he asked. "But then," the student asked naïvely, "what happens if the tree should fall down and the vine should wither and die?" The old monk laughed heartily and walked away but assured the youngster that some day he would understand when he meets the second teacher. Many years later the student met the second teacher, who was known as the One-Eyed Dragon, and told him the story of his early encounter. One-Eyed Dragon assured him that the old monk had been quite right in his teaching—"Only he missed, in you, someone who really understood his mind." "But then," the student went on, "what is the sermon? What does happen when the tree falls down and the vine dies and withers away?" "You make your old Master laugh once more," the One-Eyed Dragon smiled. Thereupon the student, at last, comprehended the whole matter and exclaimed, "there was a dagger in the old monk's laughter, after all."

In this story we see clearly that inner experience can be communicated from one person to another, but it requires the same nature of experience be shared between them. In the first instance, when the student hears the laughter of his teacher, his mind was still full of ideas of existence and nonexistence, of trees and wisteria, money and distances. Indeed, he is in a prison of words and doctrines. His own nature was heavily covered over by all these things and was incapable of grasping immediately the reality at hand. He could not grasp that which was behind the laughter. He took the laughter merely as a laughter. In the Taoist expression, he heard "the music of Earth" as "Music of Earth." However, when he heard the enigmatical confirmation of the first teacher by the second as renewing the first master's laughter, his mind was opened and the same remark immediately became the medium of communicating spiritual enlightenment. By this time he understood that there was more to the laughter then he knew at first. The Taoist would say that he heard the Heavenly music in the music of Earth. To hear the music of Heaven in the music of Earth is thus poetically expressed by the Ch'annist:

When the wild birds sing their melodies from the tops of
*   the trees,*
They carry the thoughts of the Patriarch.

When the mountain flowers are blooming,
The genuine meaning comes along with their fragrance.

The genuine meaning in the fragrance of blossoms and the Patriarch's teaching in the melodies of birds are there all the time. But a man whose mind is shut up is not aware of it. Only a man whose mind is prepared will be awakened by the fragrance of the flowers and the melodies of the birds. In such awakening complete identification of subjective and objective reality takes place. Subjectivity is objectivity and objectivity is subjectivity. There is perfect unimpeded underlying harmony between them. Furthermore, from the point of view of subjectivity there is neither attachment to it-

self nor to objectivity. To identify completely with objectivity and yet to be entirely free from it is nonattachment to either the form or the void.

To reach nonattachment the technique of "beyond
opposites" was used to open the mind. This concrete
method was further developed by the Ch'annists in
form of the *kung-an:* One day a monk came to the monastery. The master asked him whether he had been
here before. The answer was "no." The master said:
"Have a cup of tea." Later, another man who had been
there before came to see the master. Again the answer
was: "Have a cup of tea." Thereupon a monk of the
monastery asked the master: "How is it that you give
the same answer to these two men regardless of differing circumstances? For the one who has been here and
the one who has not been here your answer is, "Have a
cup of tea." The master immediately called his name,
saying: "Have a cup of tea."

"Have a cup of tea" is uniformly applied to the
differently conditioned questioners. This technique of
"beyond opposites" transcends the dichotomy of this
and that and penetrates directly to the center of being.

However, this instantaneous opening of the mind
through a *kung-an* is often beyond one's control; one
may achieve it or may fail to achieve it. Therefore, besides this direct concrete approach toward self-realization, we also find a step-by-step procedure used by
both Taoists and Buddhists. This is the logical process
of negation of negation, which leads gradually to a
deeper understanding; but it cannot guarantee the
opening up of the mind. Let us examine Chuang Tzu's
statement on the denial of denial:

There is beginning, there is no beginning. There is no no-beginning. There is being, there is non-being. There is no non-being. When suddenly there is a distinction between being and non-being, I do not know which is really being and which is really non-being. I have just made an assertion but I do not know whether something was really asserted or not really asserted.[10]

In the first section of the statement the logical process of negation of negation is described which, in Lao Tzu's words, is the process of "losing and losing." The second section points out the experience of nonattachment to either being or nonbeing, to either assertion or nonassertion, which is the Middle Way. This Middle Way is achieved through denial of denial, as clearly stated in the first section. When one has reached the second denial, one is not only free from the attachment to being, but also free from nonbeing. If one can experience this liberation from both being and nonbeing, instead of understanding it merely intellectually, one is enlightened.

It is interesting to compare this process of denial of denial to the well-known "Double Truth on Three Levels" given by Chi Tsang, the great Buddhist of the sixth century. By step-by-step negation, Chi Tsang leads us from what is common truth to what is real truth, and thus eventually to enlightenment.

The common people take all things for *yu* (being) and know nothing about *wu* (non-being). But the Buddhists told them that actually all things are *wu* and empty. Thus, on this level, to say that all things are *yu* is the common truth and to say that all things are *wu* is the higher sense of truth.

[10] *The Works of Chuang Tzu,* Chapter II, translated by Y. L. Feng with my alteration.

When we ascend to the second level, to say that all is *yu* is to look at things one-sidedly. But to say that all things are *wu* is similarly one-sided. Actually, what is *yu* is simultaneously *wu*. On this second level, then, of double truth, to say that all things are *yu* and to say that all things are *wu* are both equally common sense. One now ought to say that a "non-One-Sided Middle Path" consists in understanding that things are neither *yu* nor *wu*. That now becomes the higher sense of truth.

But on the third level, to say that absolute truth consists of what is not one-sided, means that we are making distinctions, and all distinctions are by their nature one-sided. Therefore, on this level, to say that things are neither *yu* nor *wu* is merely common sense. The higher truth consists in saying that things are neither *yu* nor *wu*, neither not-*yu* nor not-*wu*, and that the absolute truth is neither one-sided nor not one-sided.[11]

The absolute truth is achieved through denial of the denial. The truth of the first level is denied on the second. The truth of the second level is further denied on the third. The Absolute Truth of the third level is neither one-sided nor not-one-sided, neither assertion nor nonassertion. Thus enlightenment is achieved through the Middle Way. The "Double Truth on Three Levels" formulated by Chi Tsang is more systematized than the "Denial of the Denial" set forth by Chuang Tzu in a simple statement. But both of these logical processes lead to the Middle Way. When we find a Buddhist saying that nonexistence is existence and existence is nonexistence, we feel that in the utterance of ultimate verities the great minds of the Buddhists and Taoists meet.

The process of the denial of denial was not only adopted by the Middle Way School of Buddhism, but

[11] Y. L. Feng, *The Brief History of Chinese Philosophy*, pp. 245-246.

also used by *Wei-shih* or the School of Mere Ideation
to achieve enlightenment. The School classified psychic functions into various kinds of consciousnesses, or
vijñānas, the purification of which, they said, leads to
enlightenment. This process of purification is really a
process of denial: first the internal ego and external
things are denied and then the existence even of consciousness is denied. Let us take a closer view of the
system developed by the School of Mere Ideation.

According to *Wei-shih* our mental hierarchy is cate-
gorized into eight kinds of consciousnesses or *vijñānas,*
to each of which a particular function is attributed.
What we experience in the ordinary way comes
through the perception of the five senses and the sixth
consciousness. The five senses are sight, hearing, smell,
taste, and bodily sensations. The sixth, or *mano
vijñāna,* is the sense which corresponds to the intellect,
whose function is to analyze and synthesize whatever
has been first perceived by the senses. The seventh,
mana vijñāna, is the most difficult to define. On the one
hand, it functions as an ego-consciousness and serves as
a communicating agent between the sixth and eighth,
or *mano vijñāna* and *ālaya vijñāna.* On the other hand,
the seventh consciousness possesses the function of
the cosmic consciousness, which is the pure consciousness, sometimes called *agada,* or the ninth consciousness. In short, the seventh *vijñāna* is conceptual when
it is attached to the tangible, and it is illuminable
when it is intangible. The eighth consciousness, *ālaya
vijñāna,* is the storehouse for the preceding seven and
indiscriminately contains all levels of consciousness expressed by the metaphor of two kinds of seeds: the
tainted and untainted. These seeds are engendered or

stimulated by all other seven consciousnesses, and, in turn, these seeds make their sevenfold functions possible. Tainted seeds give birth to tainted *dharmas,* which, in turn, engender tainted seeds. Because of this cycle of cause and effect, man's life is caught in an endless torrent, in which the highest sense of harmony seems impossible to achieve. The School of Mere Ideation tried to solve the problem of man's predicament by transforming tainted seeds into untainted, thereby making the realm of *ālaya vijñāna* infinite and sublime.

Their well-known five progressive stages toward ultimate enlightenment are the following: Man's liberation from delusion begins with the denial of the internal ego and external things. In the correction of this dual belief in the ego and the universe we see the viewpoint of the *mahayana* philosophy adopted, which holds that aside from our consciousness there is no real ego nor universe. Everything that seems real is inseparable from our consciousness. In the second stage the intellectual understanding of mere ideation is extended and nonexistence of ego and universe are accepted in a more detailed way. In the third stage one experiences the immediacy of nondiscrimination and abides in the real and transcendental nature of mere consciousness. His mind is divorced from the differentiation of subject and object. In the fourth stage, through continuing cultivation of nondifferentiation, the tainted seeds are transformed into untainted ones. Thus supreme enlightenment is achieved and one is said to enter Nirvana. In the fifth stage all untainted seeds are harvested after their thorough transformation. What is contained in *ālaya,* the storehouse, is sublime and infinite. Since all tainted elements have been forever eliminated, all eight consciousnesses are now entirely transformed and purified, and with this purification has come enlightenment.

The five stages set forth by the School of Mere Ideation are in essence a process of negation of negation and finally lead to nondifferentiation, the ultimate reality between existence and nonexistence, which is the Middle Way. In the second chapter of *Tao Te Ching* we read: "Being and nonbeing create one another. . . . Therefore the wise deals with it by non-interference and teaches non-verbal assertion (to either side)." In essence this means that it is the Middle Path that leads to serenity. To achieve the Middle Path one must free oneself from being and nonbeing, life and death, construction and destruction. In this connection I am quoting again a passage from Chuang Tzu:

Non-po Tzu-kuei asked Nu-yü: "You are of a high age and yet your complexion is that of a child. How can that be done?" The latter answered: "I have achieved *Tao*." Then Nu-yü went on to explain: "There was Po Liang-I who had the talents of a genius, but lacked *Tao* to be a perfect man. . . . I tried to teach him so that he might become one. In three days he was able to free himself from the world. In another seven days he was free from all externalities. And in another nine days he was free from his own existence. Being free from his own existence, Nu-yü continued, he had a vision of the rising sun. After that he was able to experience Oneness. After that there was no more distinction of past and present. Then he reached the state wherein there is neither living nor dying. Then he knew that the destruction of life did not mean death, and that birth did not mean life. He dealt with everything and accepted everything. All things proceed to destruction and all things proceed to construction. This is called tran-

quilization in confusion. Tranquilization in confusion
means achievement through chaos (*Ch. VI*).

This story is Chuang Tzu's way of saying that eman-
cipation from the bondage of the ever-changing world,
from the relative value of external things, and from
the unstable and evasive existence is achieved through
the denial of denial. When one is free from all condi-
tionings, one has reached the absolute moment—the
Middle Way in which "destruction of life does not
mean death" and "birth does not mean life"; where
destruction is construction and construction is destruction.

Let us compare the steps given by Chuang Tzu to
the four *dhyanas* of the Buddhist *Lankavatara Sutra*.
The first *dhyana* teaches discard of the world because
it is impermanent, defiled, and full of suffering. The
second *dhyana* tells man to transcend external things
by contemplative examination since they are mutually
conditioned. The third *dhyana* requires man to free
himself from the two forms of nonatmanness (ego of
persons and ego of things), in order to achieve oneness. In the last *dhyana* the blissful state of Boddhi is
finally reached and one will be engaged in works for all
sentient beings. The explanations of the *dhyanas* in
the Buddhist system do not exactly correspond to
those of the steps given by Chuang Tzu. However,
both Taoist and Buddhist are applying the process of
the denial of denial in their search for the ultimate.
But we must not lose sight of the fact that the final
break-through can only come by one's most fundamental faculty innate in each of us. It is not until we
have completely freed ourselves from all condition-

ings and limitations that we can see "the rising sun."

To see the rising sun is illumination and with it one's whole being is transformed and remodeled. Psychologically speaking, it is the transformation from "a consciousness limited to ego-form in the form of the non-ego-like-self." [12] Let us listen to C. G. Jung's explanation:

> The illusion regarding the nature of self is the common confusion of the ego with self . . . Pan Shan, who says, "The world of the mind encloses the whole universe in its light," adding, "It is a cosmic life and a cosmic spirit, and at the same time an individual life and an individual spirit."
>
> However one may define self, it is always something other than the ego, and inasmuch as a higher understanding of the ego leads on to self the latter is a thing of wider scope, embracing the knowledge of the ego and therefore surpassing it. In the same way as the ego is certain knowledge of my self, so is the self a knowledge of my ego, which, however, is no longer experienced in the form of a broader or higher ego, but in the form of a non-ego (*Nicht-Ich*).
>
> . . . The occurrence of *satori* is interpreted and formulated as a break-through of a consciousness limited to ego-form in the form of the non-ego-like-self. This conception answers to the nature of Zen. . . .[13]

The transformation of the self from the ego-form to the nonego-form is the fundamental goal of both Taoism and Buddhism, and *satori* (in Japanese), or *wu* (in Chinese) is the expression of the inner awakening and transformation. The traditional interpretation of this inner experience, no matter how penetrating and direct, is often beyond our comprehension. The above

[12] C. G. Jung's Foreword to D. T. Suzuki, *An Introduction to Zen Buddhism*, p. 13.
[13] C. G. Jung's Foreword to D. T. Suzuki, *An Introduction to Zen Buddhism*, pp. 13-14.

statement is based upon subjective inner experience and conveyed by scientific description from objective observation. This scientific presentation brings out the real value of self-transformation as taught by ancient Chinese philosophers, which was left unexplained for many thousand years.

The daily lives of those who have achieved such inner experience, or enlightenment, do not differ from those of ordinary men. The ordinary man wears his clothes and eats his meals, and so does the man of enlightenment. According to Lao Tzu, he will not deal with worldly activities nihilistically:

As for where one stays, one values the proper place.
For the mind, one values its profundity.
For the friend, one values his kindness.
For words, one values sincerity.
For government, one values good order.
For affairs, one values ability.
For action, one values timeliness (Ch. VIII).

The attitude of the Taoist is in no way a nihilistic one, but rather a proper adjustment derived from the highest level of inner serenity after the transformation of his whole being. In fact, this inner serenity of the nonegolike-self creates the glories of the world that speak of the unlimited potentialities of man. In the realm of the nonegolike-self the mutual conditioning of the "gold and lion" is in perfect harmony and the dichotomy of reality and appearance is no more. In other words, man has reached the ground from which all great creativity springs. When we become aware of this "deep underlying harmony" we will truly understand the great contributions Taoists have made to the life and culture of the Eastern world.

4 Processes of self-realization

○ According to Taoism there are two routes leading to enlightenment, *ming* or ontological insight, *ching* or quiescence. The previous chapters on Sympathy, Creativity, and Peace all deal with *ming*. This chapter is devoted to the approach of *ching*.

Quiescence sometimes manifests itself as darkness. The light, we may say, emerges from darkness. We have numerous suggestions of this idea in the works of Chuang Tzu. In Chapter 22 of his canon Nieh Chüeh asks Pei I what is the nature of *Tao*. Pei I replies thus:

If you put your body in the correct posture and concentrate on the One, the Heavenly harmony will descend upon you. Hold on to your inner awareness and unify yourself with the Absolute. God will lodge within you, and you will abide with *Tao*. This achievement will fill you with joy. You will be like the newly born calf, gazing but not seeking anything.

Even while he was speaking Pei I realized that Nieh Chüeh was drifting off into the depth of quiescence.

Pei I was greatly pleased that his words had had such an immediate and overwhelming effect and went off singing:

Like a dry skeleton is his frame;
Like sparkless ashes is his mind.
Genuine is his knowledge, solid and true,
Not supported by reasoning.
Dark and dim, he has no mind,
Not accessible to discussion.
O! Lo! What kind of person is he now?

In this story we have a good illustration of tranquillity achieved through quiescence. This really is the same state that the Buddhists refer to as *samādhi*. Intellection and reasoning, all consciousness indeed, have vanished, and only the awareness of serenity remains. To banish intellection from consciousness is a process of negation. But in tranquillity we find a fuller and deeper expression, which in itself is positive and leads to enlightenment. As Chuang Tzu says in Chapter 23:

When man is extremely tranquil, then the Heavenly Light is given forth. He who emits this Heavenly Light sees his Real Self. He who cultivates his Real Self achieves the Absolute. When he achieves the Absolute the human elements will drop away, but the Heavenly qualities will come to his assistance.

These Heavenly qualities are described by Chuang Tzu who, when speaking of the great master Lao Tzu says that he sat still like a motionless corpse, and yet revealed himself as a dragon. From profound stillness a sound came forth as thunder, as if issuing from all Heaven and Earth.

To reveal one's spirit as a dragon is to say symbolically that man has achieved enlightenment. The light that shines out from a being so spiritual Chuang Tzu refers to as the dragon. Tranquillity itself is merely negative, intellection and reasoning are stripped away; but when its positive aspect is revealed it becomes the consciousness of the unconscious, a pure light shining.

This achievement of enlightenment through meditation is what the Taoists call *Tê*. When *Tê* is achieved one is said to have returned to one's original nature. Thus a man of *Tê* when he sits has no thought; when he walks he has no worries; in the depth of his mind nothing is contained. In other words, the man of *Tê* has attained to a higher stage of psychic integration through contemplation.

When we attempt to examine the etymological and connotative meaning of the word *Tê* we encounter many difficulties. This word *Tê*, which is closely related to the word *Tao*, is so complicated in its meaning and so allusive in its overtones that it requires extensive explanation. Often we are told that *Tê* means simply virtue, or moral conduct. However, in the Confucian Analects we find the master praising a fine horse not for its strength or beauty as we might expect, but for its *Tê*. Here the word, of course, does not mean anything like moral virtue or conduct, but rather something like innate qualities of character. Hence in *The Doctrine of the Mean* we find the statement: "Unless there be the attainment of *Tê* the perfect *Tao* cannot be realized." When Arthur Waley translated the *Tao Te Ching* he called it *The Way and Its Power. Tê,* Waley says, most closely corresponds to the English word power. According to *Shuo Wên,* the classic Chinese dictionary, which was compiled in the first century A.D., *Tê* means "to observe the mind." The connotation of the script can lead to the concept of contemplation and the power that results from it. The practice of contemplation itself can be traced back to the much earlier days of Lao Tzu himself. In Chapter 16 of the *Tao Te Ching* we have, for example, the following description:

Devote yourself to the Absolute Emptiness;
Contemplate earnestly in Quiescence.
All things are together in Action,
But I look into their Non-action,
For things are continuously moving, restless,[1]
Yet each is proceeding back to its origin.
Proceeding back to the origin means Quiescence.
To be in Quiescence is to see "Being-for-itself."[2]

---

[1] The Chinese phrase that I render "continuously moving, restless," is *yün yün*. Usually this is rendered in English as growing or flourishing but it is also used to indicate the opposite of quiet. The interpretation of flourishing was begun by Ho Shang Kung, who commented, *"yün yün* is the flourishing of blossoms and leaves." The later interpretation, moving and restless, which I consider more correct, is well authenticated, as in the *Yu P'ien*, or *Graphic Dictionary of Ku Yeh-wang* (A.D. 519-581), which declares that in the book of Lao Tzu *yün yün* means "not being peaceful and quiet." (See the section *Yün* in the Supplementary Volume). After all, the word *wu* (things) is the subject of the sentence and the verb can scarcely be limited to that which "blossoms and puts forth leaves," even metaphorically.

[2] *Ming*, which I translate broadly as "being-for-itself," is often rendered as life, fate, destiny, etc. Here it refers to other than material and static things. According to the commentary of *Tao Te Ching*, written by Tê Ch'ing of the sixteenth century, *ming* means self-nature. However, Su Ch'ê (eleventh century) and Chiao Kung (late sixteenth century), both famous commentators on Lao Tzu, interpret *ming* as "the wonder within the nature of things." "The nature of things we can describe, but for the wonder of the nature of things we can find no words to describe it."

I have preferred in this translation to resort to Hegel's concept of "being-for-itself." Hegel says: "Inasmuch as the 'state or condition' is cancelled through change, change itself also is cancelled. Being, consequently, with this process, has gone back into itself and excludes otherness from itself. It is *For Itself*. . . . This excluding is at the

"Being-for itself" is the all-changing-changeless. [3]
To understand the all-changing-changeless is to be en-
  lightened.
Not to know that, but to act blindly, leads to disaster.
The all-changing-changeless is all-embracing.[4]
To embrace all is to be selfless.[5]
To be selfless is to be all-pervading.[6]
To be all-pervading is to be transcendent.[7]

This passage from the *Tao Te Ching* contains a
clear description of what a Man of *Tê* is, because it follows in progressive detail the process of contemplation,
which is from action to nonaction: the reverse of the
usual course of psychic functions. Through nonaction
absolute quietude is achieved. One sees one's own original nature, and when this occurs one interfuses with
the ten thousand things and becomes one of them. This
interfusion of one's self and the ten thousand things is
all-pervading and all-embracing. In this state one is
selfless. Thus, we say, one is in the realm of nonbeing,

---

same time a bringing-into-relation to others, and hence it is likewise
an attracting." (See the *Philosophical Propaedeutics,* translated by
William T. Harris.) Hegel's phrase seems to come closest to the concept of the "wonder of the nature of things" as the idea is conceived
by Su Ch'ê and Chiao Kung.

[3] Ch'ang, the "all-changing changeless," presents one of the basic
concepts of Taoism. The word *ch'ang* may be translated constant,
permanent, unceasing, eternal, etc., i.e., the opposite of changing.
Lao Tzu says: "Soundless, formless, existing by itself and unchanging," in referring to *Tao.* And Chuang Tzu says: "Before heaven and
earth were, *Tao* existed by itself from all time. . . . No point in
time is long ago, nor by the lapse of ages has it grown old." However, Taoists do accept the observable fact that things *do* change all
the time. *Ch'ang* is what is unchanging in all changes.

[4] *Jung,* all-embracing.

[5] *Kung,* selfless.

[6] *Wang,* all-pervading.

[7] *T'ien,* transcendent. These four words (*Jung, Kung, Wang, T'ien*)
describe the stages of contemplation, or quietness, after the achievement of enlightenment. In the realm of the absolute void there is
interfusion and interpenetration of self and others, man and the universe. Such interfusion and interpenetration take place naturally and
inevitably.

or void. This, too, of course, is the basic goal of Yoga.

Yoga, as the Indian philosophers interpret it, is a way of abstract meditation (*samādhi*) and transcendental wisdom (*prajna*). "These two means are like two bullocks tied to the yoke of a cart and drawing it to its destination." [8] From the earliest Chinese records we have and from the works of Chuang Tzu and Lao Tzu as they have been handed down to us we know that "abstract meditation" was practiced in the early days by the Taoists, and that transcendental wisdom was achieved by them. Closely connected with meditation, the consequence of which is wisdom, are the breathing techniques ordinarily associated with Yoga.

In China meditative breathing exercises were also practiced for the attainment of *Tao*. We find, for example, even in an early poem by Ch'u Yüan (died c.a. 288 B.C.), entitled "Wandering in the Distance," a suggestion of a technique for the achievement of *Tao* through controlled breathing. The poem, freely translated, reads:

Eat six kinds of air and drink pure dew in order to preserve the purity of the soul. Breathe in the essence of the air and breathe the foul air out. The *Tao* is minute and without content, and yet it is large and without limit. Do not confuse your soul—it will be spontaneous. Concentrate on the breath and *Tao* will remain with you in the middle of the night.

To return to the Taoist works, we find other references to meditative breathing as an aid to the attainment of transcendental wisdom. In Chapter 10 of the

[8] Sarvepalli Radhakrishnan: *History of Philosophy: Eastern and Western*, p. 180. George Allen and Unwin, London, 1952.

Tao Te Ching, Lao Tzu discusses breathing exercises in connection with meditation:

Can you concentrate on your breathing to reach harmony
And become as an innocent babe?
Can you clean the Dark Mirror[9] within yourself
And make it of perfect purity? . . .

To achieve inner harmony Lao Tzu himself recommends breathing exercises for concentration and purification. The idea of the adoption of breathing exercises in order to attain to transendental wisdom is referred to by Chuang Tzu as *hsin chai* or fasting mind. He describes it in Chapter IV of his work as follows:

Concentrate on the goal of meditation.
Do not listen with your ear but listen with your mind;
Not with your mind but with your breath.
Let hearing stop with your ear,
Let the mind stop with its images.
Breathing means to empty oneself and to wait for Tao.
Tao *abides only in the emptiness.*
This emptiness is the fasting mind. . . .
Look at the Void! In its chamber light is produced.
Lo! Joy is here to stay.

These passages which I have just quoted present strong evidence of the fact that breathing exercises were recommended and practiced even in the earliest Taoist teaching. The ancient Chinese philosophers realized that breathing techniques could be used to

---

[9] The dark mirror-mind. Chuang Tzu says: "The perfect man's mind is like a mirror. . . . It reflects things but does not retain them." A more literal translation of the two lines might be "Clean the dark mirror and let no stain remain," which sounds similar to the famous *gatha* made by Shen-hsiu (d. 706): "The mind is like a bright mirror; clean it from time to time and let it retain no dust."

fortify the process of meditation. Thus in the works of Chuang Tzu we find the declaration that the perfect man breathes "through his heels" while the ordinary man breathes through his throat, another concrete reference to the probability that the Chinese had developed their own system of breathing exercises. However, in Chapter 15 Chuang Tzu warns against the reliance upon mere physical exercises, breathing or otherwise, without the study and application of Taoist philosophy. Without a real comprehension of the philosophy such disciplines will have no efficacy in achieving transcendental wisdom. Here is the passage:

When man breathes in and out, or inhales and exhales in order to release the old air and take in the new, man hibernates like a bear and stretches his neck like a bird, he is merely striving for longevity. Such a man indulges in breathing exercises in order to develop his physique, wishing to live as long as Peng Tzu. . . . If one achieves longevity, not through breathing, but through the emptiness of the mind—forgetting everything and possessing nothing—he has reached purity and infinity. All good qualities come along with it. This is the *Tao* of Heaven and Earth.

According to the Taoists, breathing exercises may facilitate the attainment of spiritual wisdom, but its actual realization is the spontaneous awakening of the pure consciousness, from the center of one's innermost being. This pure inner consciousness is not esoteric, available only to a few, but is universal, innate in all. However, not every one of us is conscious of possessing it. As for its general characterization, it is not inferential or rationalistic, but immediate and primordial. It leaves no trace, but indicates the significance of

the absolute moment, disregarding space and time.
The experience of it comes only from the highest level
of one's own nature. To achieve it is to free oneself
from the bondage of the limitations of the finite mind
and to gain an insight into one's innermost being. The
following passage from the works of Chuang Tzu,
Chapter VI, describes the attainment of such spiritual
freedom:

In three days he was able to free himself from the world.
Having no regard for the world, in another seven days he
was able to free himself from all externalities. And again,
after another nine days, he was able to free himself from
his own existence. Being free from his own existence, he
had the vision of the "rising sun." After that he was able to
experience Oneness. After that, there was no distinction of
past and present. Then he reached the state wherein there
is neither living nor dying. Then he knew that the destruction of life did not mean death, and that birth did
not mean life. He dealt with everything and accepted
everything. To him all things proceed to destruction and
all things proceed to construction. This is called tranquilization in confusion. Tranquilization in confusion means
achievement through chaos.

In this passage we see that the Taoist first transcends
worldly affairs, then material things, and finally even
his own existence. Through this step-by-step nonattachment he achieves enlightenment and is able to see
all things as One. He is then free from all conditioning,
past or present, life or death, destruction or construction. Nothing of that kind can confuse him. Thus he
reaches tranquillity, the highest level of integration. In
other words, the higher level of integration is obtained by freeing oneself from all confusion. This is
what Lao Tzu calls "The Method of Losing." He says:

"To search for knowledge is to gain day by day; to search for *Tao* is to lose day by day." By losing and losing one ultimately reaches the state of nonaction. When one achieves nonaction one is enlightened, free from differentiations and distinctions. One sees the one and becomes part of the one. The method is more completely described by Chuang Tzu, Chapter VI, in the following story:

Once Yen Huei, a student of Confucius, reported to the Master that he was making progress. He said "I forget the moral distinction of benevolence and righteousness." The Master said: "Good, but not perfect." Another day Yen Huei said: "I forget rituals and music." The Master said: "Very well, but still not perfect." The third time this earnest student came to the Master, saying: "I forget myself while sitting." The Master was surprised and asked: "What do you mean, that you forget yourself while sitting?" The student answered: "It is to free oneself from the bodily form and to disregard hearing and seeing. Through the transcendence of the bodily form and the elimination of sensations one identifies oneself with the Infinite. This is what I mean by forgetting myself while sitting."

The authenticity of this story about Confucius and his disciple as told by a Taoist master has been questioned by later Confucianists. However, the teaching of self-forgetfulness to achieve enlightenment in meditation as described here is very important in Taoist doctrine. This is really the basic idea of Lao Tzu's doctrine of *sun chih yu sun* or "losing and losing." Both the technique of "losing and losing" as suggested by Lao Tzu and Chuang Tzu's *tso wang* or "forgetting self by sitting" were not only practiced by the Taoists, but were also used by early Chinese Buddhists to explain

the teaching of Indian Yoga. In the introduction to the
Sutra on Breathing by the famous Buddhist master,
Tao-an (312-285), we find the following passage:

The breathing technique known as *Ānāpāna* refers to
the inhaling and exhaling of the breath. *Tao* and *Tê* rest
in all places; there is no place that they are not to be found.
Ānāpāna is the use of breathing to achieve inward integration. There are four meditation techniques which make
use of the functions of the body. Through breathing exercises we pass through the six stages toward integration.
Bodily exercises lead through four steps toward concentration. These steps consist of "losing and losing" until we
have reached *wu wei* or non-action, or "forgetting and
forgetting" until we have done away with all desire. By
non-action we come into accord with things. By non-desire
harmony comes in our affairs. By being in accord with
things we can see into their nature. Through harmony in
our affairs we can accomplish our missions. Accomplishing
our missions, we make all that is, consider itself as the
other. Seeing into the nature of things, we cause the whole
world to forget self. Thus we eliminate the other and we
eliminate the self. This is to achieve integration into the
One.

Although this was written by a Buddhist scholar,
Tao-an, his philosophy of meditative breathing bears
a striking resemblance to that taught by the Taoist masters Lao Tzu and Chuang Tzu. It is not just a matter
of using their terminology, but it seems that the very
method employed and the goal of meditation are essentially the same in Buddhism and Taoism. So that the
methods of "losing and losing" and "forgetting and forgetting" in the Taoist classics are not merely meant to
identify the Buddhist terms, but they are rather an indication of a common fundamental approach to enlightenment.

However, when we take a closer view, we notice that the Indian and the Chinese systems of Yoga differ considerably. This can be explained by the fact that each of them built upon its own philosophical framework. The Taoist system of meditative breathing was a product of its native ground. We not only have the works of Lao Tzu and Chuang Tzu, but many other roots. There is, for example, the well-known *I Ching,* or *Book of Changes,* and the widely prevalent theories of the Five Elements, as well as the principles of *yin-yang* and the work of the Chinese alchemists, numerologists, and prognosticators. Above all, there were the Chinese cosmological theories and the macrocosmic-microcosmic view of man as the universe contained in the individual.

The fundamental—or at any rate the earliest—Taoist text on meditative breathing is the work entitled *T'san-t'ung-ch'i,* or *Meditation on Identity and Unity* (ca. 142). It was the work of Wei-Pe-yang. The book became famous for commentaries written by Chu Hsi in the twelfth century and Yü Yen in the thirteenth century.

The basic idea of the work, as Yü Yen stated it in his introduction, is that "if man seizes for himself the secret forces of Heaven and Earth in order thereby to compound for himself the great elixir of the golden fluid, he will then exist coeval with Heaven and Earth from the beginning. . . . Each time that Heaven unites itself with the Earth seize for yourself the secret springs of the creative activities of *yin* and *yang.*" To rephrase this, we might say that to seize the secret force of the macrocosmic universe for application to the microcosmic universe of man, is a matter of compounding an inner elixir.

The basic theory of this Inner Elixir School, as it is known, is that the inner elixir is compounded through *ching* (essence), *ch'i* (breath), and *shên* (spirit). It is hard to identify these words precisely in English. According to the Taoist, each of these three principles involves two aspects. One is material, visibly manifested, the other invisible primordial power from the universe. The former functions inwardly in man, the latter outwardly in Heaven and Earth. For example, *ching,* or essence, in its material form is sperm. Therefore Taoist meditative practice draws its power through the spine and is said to commence from the Gate of the Tail. Sperm provides the vitality of the human body, maintaining energy and life. But *ching* cannot be complete without an understanding of its immaterial, primordial aspect. In this light it is not sperm at all, but an invisible, ungraspable cosmic force that derives from something outside the universe, such as the sun and the moon. It is said that through breathing man takes in this cosmic force for the compounding of the inner elixir.

As for *ch'i*, breath, it is, in one sense, the physical effort of the beginning practitioner, who inhales and exhales, moving his diaphragm up and down. But when the practitioner achieves embryo breathing he is said to be in the state of total extinction, or cessation. It is the primordial beginning of the universe. In man it is referred to as breathing without breath. This is called embryo breathing or primordial breathing. From it man draws the invisible, ungraspable force of the universe for compounding the elixir.

The third principle, *shên,* refers to both *shih shên,* or ordinary consciousness, and *yuan shên,* or spiritual consciousness. The former is man's senses, perceptions, thoughts, feelings, and the like, which are obtained at birth or afterward. The latter is the spiritual consciousness existing before one is born. As soon as man is born, it becomes invisible, covered by man's ordinary consciousness. It is believed that through meditation man can once again reveal this spiritual consciousness and eliminate his ordinary consciousness. What is this primordial spiritual consciousness? It is a part of the power that permeates and pervades the whole universe.

All three elements, *ching, ch'i,* and *shên,* refer to one thing, which contains no form and has no color. They are fundamental to the human, since all three lead to the inner elixir. There is a Taoist Yogin motto which goes: *Lien ching hua ch'i, lien ch'i hua shên.* That is:

Through compounding sperm (*ching*), the breath (*ch'i*) is transformed; through compounding the breath, the spirit (*shên*) is transformed. Thus *ching, ch'i,* and *shên* are most fundamental elements in the process of meditative breathing.

However, the Taoist practitioner further emphasizes that to compound the spirit means to return to nothingness or void. The Chinese expression is, *Lien shên fu hsü. Hsü* means nonbeing, or nothingness. Before man is born this phenomenon of nonbeing is basically unique, but as soon as man is born, this unique force separates into two: *ming* (life or destiny) and *hsing* (the spiritual nature of man). In other words, *ming* is the substance of life and death, *hsing* is the root of spiritual consciousness. *Ming* is the beginning of *ch'i,* or breath. Yet *ming* itself is not *ch'i,* but is where *ch'i* is produced. *Hsing* is the beginning of spiritual consciousness, yet it itself is not spiritual consciousness, but it is where the spiritual consciousness of man has its origin.

This seems to say that *ming* connotes material form and *hsing* connotes spiritual function. However, the divergence in viewpoint here on the part of the Taoists and the Neo-Confucianists is very great. Nevertheless, we can say that the central principle of Taoist meditative practice is to unify these two elements—conscious spirit and substantial ether—toward the attainment of oneness, which, in turn, is nothingness, nonbeing. The practitioner says he compounds spirit to return to nonbeing.

The Taoist uses these concepts of *hsing* and *ming* as the basis for his breathing theory. These two represent, so to speak, ways of psychic circulation. Through deep breathing one lengthens one's life span, or *ming.* Substance is transformed. Through concentration on nothingness, one awakens his cosmic consciousness to spiritual revelation. Thus by cultivating both substance and spirit in meditation one dissolves one's self in the macrocosmic force and becomes part of it.

It is obvious that the theory of Taoist meditation is based upon a view of man as a microcosmic universe, reflecting the macrocosmic universe about him. The movement of the inner and outer worlds is intimately correlated. Outwardly man moves with the vast forces of the Heaven and Earth; inwardly there is the functioning of his own organs, following their universal pattern. Thus the physical functions and the structure of the inner organs have their cosmic analogies. It is on these cosmic analogies that the Taoist system of meditative breathing is constructed.

The earliest Taoist classic based on this system of analogies is the work known as the *Huai-nan-tzu*, which dates from the second century B.C. This work discusses the place of man in the universe as a background to a system of meditative breathing. We read:

> What is spiritual is received from Heaven while the body and its material form are derived from the Earth. It is the harmony of the spirits of *yin* and *yang* on which all harmony depends. . . .

> Heaven has four seasons, five elements, nine divisions, three hundred and sixty days. Similarly, man has four limbs, five internal organs, nine orifices and three hundred and sixty joints. Heaven has wind, rain, cold, heat; man, similarly, has joy, anger, taking, giving. . . . Man forms a trinity with Heaven and Earth, and his mind is the master. . . . In the Sun there is a bird standing on three legs, and in the Moon a toad with three legs. . . .

Man, thus, is a microcosmic universe. This idea occurs frequently, indeed constantly, in Taoism, and the meditative breathing school proves no exception in using this concept for its own purposes. Through meditative breathing man achieves the natural integration of self with the universe. This integration is destined for him and forshadowed in many ways, according to the early Taoist writings.

Based upon this idea of universal identification, the Taoist practitioner achieves a harmony of the microcosmic universe within and harmony in his relation to the macrocosmic universe without. The macrocosmos is composed of five basic elements: wood, fire, earth, metal, and water; in the microcosmos there are five basic inner organs: kidney, liver, lung, spleen, and heart. Each inner organ is identified with an element without. Also in their relation to one another the five inner organs follow the pattern of the five elements. As each element is the product of another their relationship becomes ultimately circular. This circular movement also applies to the inner organs. Early in the second century, Tung Chung-shu, a Confucianist, commenting on the system of the five elements, said:

> Heaven comprises five elements: the first is wood, the second fire, the third earth, the fourth metal, and the fifth water. Wood is the beginning of the cycle, water the last, and earth is in the center of the circle. Such is the order given by nature. Wood produces fire, fire produces earth, earth metal, metal water, water wood. This is the father-son relationship.

Tung Chung-shu further correlates the five elements to the sequence of the seasons and the directions. He continues:

> The five elements move in a circle in proper order, each of them performing its specific functions. Therefore, wood is located in the East and characterizes the *ch'i* or ether of Spring. Fire is located in the South and characterizes the *ch'i* of Summer. Metal is located in the West and characterizes the *ch'i* of Autumn. Water is located in the North and characterizes the *ch'i* of Winter. . . . Earth dwells in the center and is called Heavenly Nourisher (a natural source of nourishment for the four elements).

Ch'i, we see, is closely related to the five elements. Tung Chung-shu explains:

> When the *ch'i* in the universe is condensed, it becomes One. When it is divided, we have *yin* and *yang*. When it is quartered we have the four seasons. When it is further

divided we have the five elements. Each element has its own movement. On account of this difference in movement, we speak of the five movers.

When the five movers move outside in the universe, we have wood, fire, earth, metal and water; but when they act within man, we have liver, heart, spleen, lung, and kidney. When they are condensed they are one. This oneness is identified as *ch'i* in the universe as well as in man.

The five movers within and without are also identified with a set of numbers. Number 1 is assigned to water; 2 to fire; 3 to wood; 4 to metal; and 5 to earth. This is the first set of symbolic numbers, which contains three odd or *yang* numbers and two even or *yin* numbers. In the second set 6 stands for water; 7 for fire; 8 for wood; 9 for metal; and 10 for earth. This set contains three even or *yin* numbers and two odd or *yang* numbers. Since the kidney is identified with water it takes numbers 1 and 6; the heart, identified with fire, takes numbers 2 and 7. The liver takes the numbers of wood, 3 and 8; the lung takes the numbers of metal, 4 and 9; the spleen takes the earth numbers, 5 and 10. Hence each organ, characterized by both odd and even numbers, contains the two qualities of *yin* and *yang*. *Yin* and *yang* circulate among the five organs; therefore, the breathing movement is a cyclical one.

This breathing circle is also illustrated by a set of trigrams from the *I Ching*. The four trigrams are *Chen*☳, indicating East; *Li* ☲, South; *Tui* ☱, West; and *K'an* ☵, North. They are embraced by a circular movement that starts from *Chen* and ends in *K'an*, there beginning a new circuit. In Appendix V to the *I Ching* we read:

All things issue forth in *Chen,* which is East. . . . *Li* suggests brightness, where all things come to see each other. This trigram represents the South. . . . *Tui* is the West and Autumn, the season in which all things are moving by their joy. . . . *K'an* refers to water. It is the trigram of the North where all things return to rest and comfort. We say "rest and comfort indicate *K'an.*"

According to the *Ts'an-Tung-ch'i* not only seasons and directions are related to one another, but also man's inner organs as well as various animals belong to this relationship. Thus *chen* finally stands for east, spring, liver and the Blue Dragon; *li* applies to south, summer, heart, and the Red Bird; *tui* denotes the west, autumn, lung, and the White Tiger; *k'an* stands for north, winter, kidney, and the Black Turtle. It is for the convenience of discussion that we have these separate centers, each identified by its various names. When breathing takes place they move along the circle. They dissolve in the movement, thus becoming a part of it. In fact, movement and movers are one.

Besides this set of four trigrams there is a fifth, which is situated at the center of the circle. However, the Taoist calls the fifth center the storage place for all the energies and the source of vital forces for the other, peripheral, centers. This fifth center is identified with the Earth and the spleen and is characterized as inner *yang* and outer *yin.* Through the movement of *yin* and *yang* it receives and radiates powers from the peripheral centers. In an apocryphal addition to the *I Ching* known as the *Yi wei Ch'ien tso tu (Apocryphal Treatise on the Changes),* commented on by Chêng Hsüan as early as the second century, we find a metaphysical category of four that was later picked up by the Taoist for his own purposes. The relevant passage in the *Yi-wei-Ch'ien-tso-tu* reads as follows:

In ancient times the Sages worked upon the principles of *yin* and *yang* to determine the principles of growth and decline, and established *Ch'ien* and *K'un* in order to govern the fundamentals of Heaven and Earth. That which has form is produced of the formless. Whence came *Ch'ien* and *K'un*? In answer we may say that first there was the Great Principle of Change, then the Great Beginning, then the Great Origin, and then the Great Simplicity.

The Yogi has, typically, added a fifth category. This is the great ultimate, the unifying whole.

In the Taoist *Sutra* we often find such expressions as "the union of *K'an* and *Li*" or "the union of Heart and Kidney," which indicates that in the inner circulation the four original categories have been simplified into two movers. East and south combine into the upper center, which is named *li*, or heart, or dragon, or Sun; and west and north combine into the lower center named *k'an*, or kidney, or tiger, or Moon. Therefore, we say, the union of *li* and *k'an*, or heart and kidney, or Sun and Moon, produces the fundamental breathing current. This is called *hsiao-chou-t'ien*, or the lesser heavenly circulation. The structure of this current is arbitrarily correlated to various categories such as the seasons, directions, animals, trigrams, inner organs, and others. Symbolic word play of this sort is, of course, subject to endless variations. The important thing is that these symbols are merely used to illustrate the breathing circulation among the inner centers of man, just as an invisible movement exists among the seasons and directions. As movement is the unifying

Fig. 1   *Centers on lesser heavenly circulation*

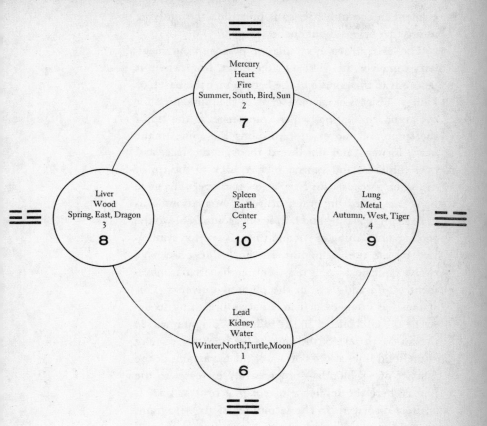

element in the universe, so is breathing the unifying means that brings about oneness in man.

The lesser heavenly circulation begins in the imaginary center of the chest, i.e., the heart, from where it descends to the middle of the belly under the navel, or kidney. This lesser current serves as the foundation for the grand circulation, which commences at the tip of the spine and moves upward along the spine to the head, forward and downward through the face, and over the chest and ventral surface back to the tip of the spine. Because this circulation goes over the entire body it is called the grand heavenly circulation. This movement is a rising and falling one, comparable to the waxing and waning of *yin* and *yang*. It is often symbolized by the twelve months. In the *I Ching* we have twelve basic hexagrams representing the circular movement of *yin* and *yang* in the physical universe. This system was often used in meditative breathing to describe the circulation. In the following diagram we see that in the pattern of the months the influence of *yang* —the solid lines at the bottom of the hexagrams in the first set of six months—progressively increases to the point where the influence of *yin* (the broken line) is entirely displaced. In the second set of six hexagrams we see that the exact reverse of this phenomenon takes place: the *yang* progressively decreases to the point where it is displaced by the *yin*. Each progressive and regressive stage of this process has a name and a corresponding month that it represents.

HEXAGRAM						
NAME:	FU	LIN	T'AI	TA-CHUANG	KUAI	CH'IEN
MONTH:	11	12	1	2	3	4
CENTER:	WEI-LU	SHUN-FU	HSÜAN-SHU	CHAI-CHI	T'AO-TAO	YU-CHEN

HEXAGRAM						
NAME:	KOU	TUN	FOU	KUAN	PO	K'UN
MONTH:	5	6	7	8	9	10
CENTER:	NI-WAN	MING-T'UNG	T'AN-CHUNG	CHUNG-HUAN	SHEN-CHUEH	CH'I-HAI

According to Chinese astrologists the *yang* movement begins with the eleventh month, which is identified with *fu*. This *yang* movement increases through the twelfth month, *lin,* up to the fourth month, *ch'ien,* when it reaches its complete dominance. At the fifth month, *kou,* the *yang* movement begins to decrease, until, when it reaches the tenth month, *yin* has gained complete dominance. On the other hand, the *yin* movement begins to decrease in the eleventh month and this decreasing movement continues until the fourth month, when *yang* has gained complete sway. At the fifth month, *kou, yin* begins to increase until at the tenth month, *k'un,* it is in turn complete.

Thus we have in the physical universe the fluctuating influence of *yin* and *yang* during the twelve months of the year. This particular idea of the waxing and waning of the physical universe was paralleled to the process of circulation in the human body. Since *yang* commences its waxing movement in the eleventh month, the Taoist adopts the hexagram *fu* as the initial point of departure for the grand circulation of the body and designates its corresponding center as the tip of the spine: *wei-lu.* This waxing or upward movement ascends through a series of specific centers along the spine. Starting at *wei-lu* it moves next to *shun-fu,* which is identified with the twelfth month, *lin,* then to *hsüan-shu,* which is the first month, *t'ai,* then to *chia-chi,* which is the second month, *ta-chuang*, then to *t'ao-tao*, the third month, *kuai*, and finally to *yu-chen*, the fourth month, *ch'ien*, when *yang* has gained complete dominance. The waxing movement of *yin* commences at *ni-wan* (top of the head) and is identified with the fifth month, *kou*, moves to *ming-t'ang*, the sixth month, *tun*, then to *t'an-chung*, the seventh month, *fou*, then to *chung-huan*, the eighth month, *kuan*, then to *shen chueh*, the ninth month, *po*, and finally to *ch'i-hai*, the tenth month, *k'un*, where *yin* reaches complete dominance. The fluctuation of *yin* and *yang* movement takes place while the breath is ascending and descending in the grand circulation.

The grand circulation of the breath throughout the body is divided into two "courses." The rising circulation from the tip of the spine, or *wei-lu*, through *shun-fu, hsüan-shu,* and the other centers to *ni-wan,* the top of the head, and then descending through *ming-t'ang* to the upper lip, is known as the *to mu,* or controlled course. The descending circulation from the lower lip through *t'ang-chung* in the chest and the other centers in the belly to the tip of the spine is known as the *jen mu,* or involuntary course. Both the involuntary and controlled courses in the grand circulation and the union of *k'an* and *li* in the lesser circulation are, as we have mentioned before, purely imaginary for the beginner. However, after a certain time and a degree of practice he may feel the circulation of the "breath" as a heat current.

This heat current is set into motion by the technique of concentration. The practitioner may focus his attention on any one of the twelve centers to start the current. The chosen center may be *ch'i-hai,* or the sea of breath, below the navel, or *wei-lu,* the tip of the spine, or *ming-t'ang,* the hall of light between the eyes, or any other. It is common practice for men to concentrate on *ch'i-hai,* while women usually concentrate on *t'ang-chung,* the center of the chest. *Ch'i-hai* is the most important center, known as the regular field of the elixir. It is the lowest of the three fields of the elixir on the path of the grand circulation. The middle field of the elixir lies in the region of the heart, and the higher field of the elixir in the top of the head. It is said to be located in the middle of the nine sections of the brain and is known also as *ni-wan,* or Nirvana. The region between the middle and the lower fields is named the yellow court, or the center of the Earth.

The drawings shown in Figure 2 are reproductions from the *Hsing-ming Chih-kuai,* or *Meaning of Nature and Destiny,* of the sixteenth century, which serve as aids to explain meditative breathing techniques. Four other illustrations from the above-mentioned book are widely known in the West since they were reproduced in Wilhelm's translation of *The Secret of the Golden Flower.* When studying these diagrams we encounter difficulties, as each center is referred to by a number of different names. Unless familiar with these synonyms one becomes easily confused. For example, the center of the higher field of elixir is alternatingly named Heavenly valley, jade pool, purple court, mystic chamber, and others. Here, in the drawing of the front view, it is called center of nature and destiny, but in the drawing of the back view primordial spirit. Both names denote the same center, the higher field of elixir.

The front view shows the centers of the involuntary course of the grand circulation. On the abdomen

Fig. 2   *Centers on grand heavenly circulation*

A. FRONT VIEW

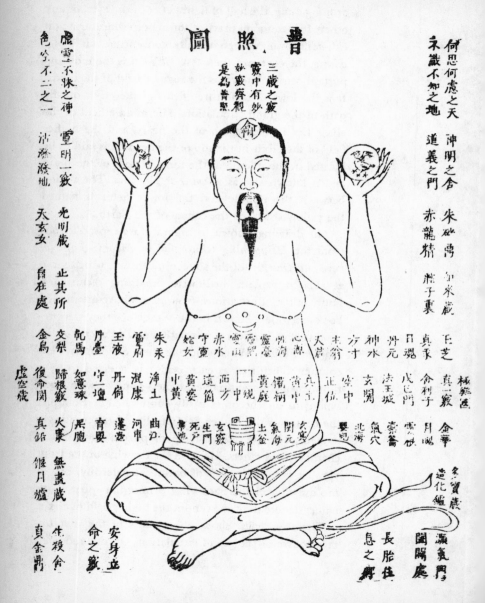

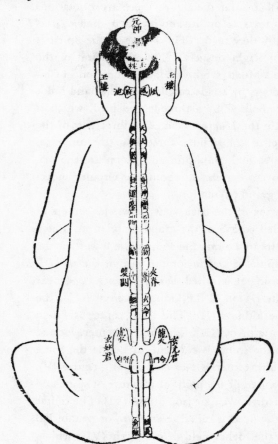

the position of the middle field of elixir is identified
by a new Moon and three stars, the yellow court by a
square, and the regular (or lower) field of elixir by a
cauldron. Two other centers, known as *t'an-chung* or
the middle of the chest, and *ming t'ang* or the hall of
light between the eyes, have not been marked in the
drawing. All around the figure there are quotations
from Taoist texts, recondite and mystic in their character. Typically they read: "The House of the Spirit is
the Door of Righteousness." The right hand of the
figure holds a Moon, symbolized, as is common in Chinese mythology, by a jade rabbit. The left hand holds
the sun, symbolized by a three-legged bird, which is
mentioned in the *Huai-nan-tzu*. The three legs of the
bird symbolize the triune forces of the universe:
Heaven, Earth and Man. Sun and Moon are the primordial movers that bring about the circular movement in the grand circulation.

The drawing of the back view shows the centers of
the controlled course of the grand circulation. These
centers are located along the spine. The lowest, at the
tip of the spine, is *wei lu*, or the gate of the tail (I).
In this drawing it is called *ch'ang ch'iang*. The next
center in the region of the kidneys is *shun fu*, or the
court of the kidneys (II). The third center is *hsuan
shu*, or mystic pivot (III). The fourth center, located
halfway up the spine, is *chia chi*, or beside the spine
(IV). The fifth center is *t'ao tao*, or jolly course (V).
The sixth center, at the point of juncture of spine and
skull, is called *yu chen*, or jade pillow (VI). The center
located in the head is called *yuan shen*, or primordial
spirit. It is the higher field of the elixir (VII) which,
as we know, has various names. Authorities differ in

their interpretations of the centers as to details and their significance.

A brief comparison of Taoist breathing "centers" with those characteristically used in Tantric Yoga may be necessary in this connection. Edward Conze in his *Buddhism: Its Essence and Development* points out that there are four main internal centers in Indian Tantric Yoga, namely, the center in the region of the navel, in the heart, in the neck, and in the head. When we examine the Chinese diagram of the centers in the grand circulation, we can easily identify these four spots. Sir John Woodroffe, in his *The Serpent Power*, speaks of six centers: "Inside the *Meru*, or spinal column, are the six main centres of *Tattvik* operations . . . *Muladhara, Svadhishthana, Manipura, Anahata, Vishuddha,* and *Ajna.*" The first is the tip of the spine, the second is in the genital region, the third is at the navel, the fourth in the center of the chest, the fifth in the throat, and the sixth between the eyes. All six obviously have corresponding centers in Chinese Taoist Yoga. The question arises, "Which of the two systems is the original one?" Conze points out that Tantric Yoga was not organized until the fifth or sixth century. It is most interesting that the Chinese work that we have mentioned, *Meditation on Identity and Unity,* published in the second century, which served as the basic text for Taoist Yoga, nowhere mentions Indian practices. Even the *Wu-chen P'ien,* the *Treatise on Enlightenment of Truth,* published about 1095, has only a few references to what we know as Indian Yoga and these are rather of an elusive nature, although later works are no doubt familiar with Indian practices. The excellent but little known *Hsing-ming Chih-kuei,* or *Meaning of Nature and Destiny,* by an unknown author, published in the sixteenth century, exhibits a complete knowledge of Indian Yoga and has a picture of Lao Tzu, Confucius, and Buddha sitting together in meditation. Much evidence suggests that Chinese Yoga developed independently during the early centuries of its existence, and that it had its own roots in ancient Chinese culture.

It is a fact that the inner centers were known to Chinese medical science many centuries before Christ. As they were closely linked to the practice of acupuncture and cauterization, they may even have been known in the remote days of the legendary Yellow Emperor, to whom tradition attributes the introduction of these practices. In the book entitled *Chinese Acupuncture and Cauterization,* published in 1956, Chan T'an-an states that meditative breathing and the inner centers were mentioned in medical works of the third and fourth centuries B.C. One of the basic medical classics, *Ling-shu,* contains twelve diagrams of man's inner centers, each with explanatory material. One of them shows the controlled course with twenty-eight centers (see Figure 3); another shows the involuntary course with twenty-four centers (see Figure 4). It is in these old medical classics that the names controlled course and involuntary course first appear. Amazingly enough, an entire chapter is devoted to the circulation of breath. The author correlates the normal as well as the abnormal functioning of the inner organs to the circulation of the breath. The basic principle of circulation is related to the fluctuations of the *yin* and *yang* forces and the transformation of the energies symbolized by the five elements.

In connection with the circulation we have to say a

Fig. 3   Centers on controlled course

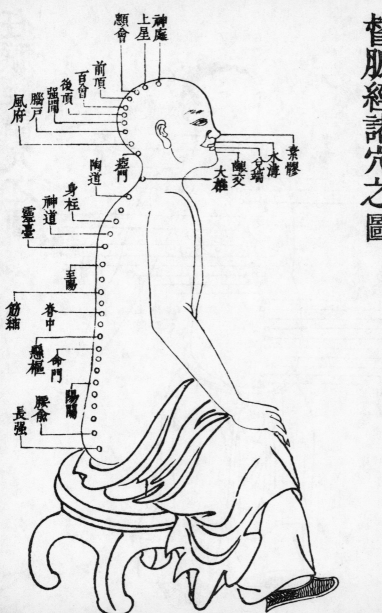

Fig. 4　*Centers on involuntary course*

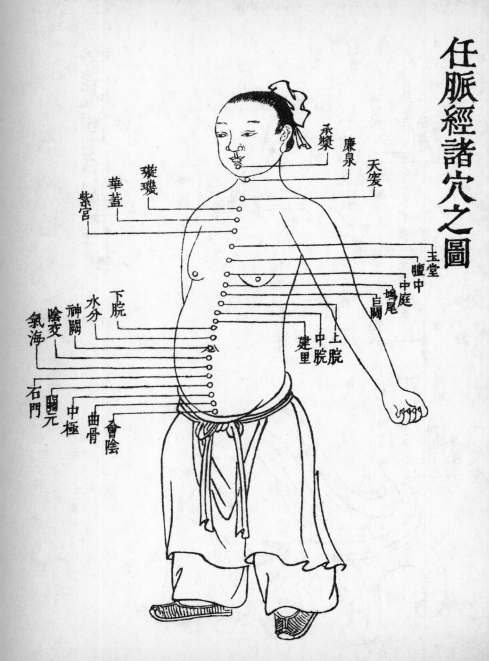

few words about the breathing technique. In Taoist
breathing a slow, deep, rhythmic inhaling and exhaling
is a basic requirement in the early stages of training.
When air is taken in, it is to be sent as deep as the abdomen. It is for this reason that the kidney center beneath the navel is called the sea of breath. When one
exhales, the diaphragm rises and the abdomen pulls
in, quite the opposite of chest breathing. The beginner counts his breaths but when his technique is more
advanced this practice is dropped.

However, just taking in air and releasing it does not
fulfill the purpose of meditative breathing. To make
it more effective, concentration is recommended. One
has to send a genuine idea along with the movement of
breathing. When inhaling, one lets the idea sink from
the heart region down to the region of the kidney or the
sea of breath. When exhaling, one brings the idea from
the tip of the spine upward along the spine and back to
the region of the heart. Thus one completes the lesser
circulation. Actually, of course, the breath cannot travel
through the spine and abdomen, but the sending of the
idea along the path of the lesser circulation is very like
breathing along this pathway. Perhaps we may refer to
this movement as a heat current that moves along the
lesser circulation by one's idea. The same is true of the
grand circulation; one leads the current by his idea
from the tip of the spine all the way upward to the top
of the head and from there one lets the current descend
through the face and chest back to the abdomen. The
ability to move this current by one's idea is acquired by
training. After a short period of concentration one feels
that one can easily send his idea to any chosen spot.
After further training one is able to feel it move along

the involuntary and controlled courses. This genuine idea can only emerge from the state of no-thought, or nonbeing, which is neither a thought nor an idea in the conventional sense. It is an inner awareness of one's concentration on the centers and the movement along the paths of the circulation. In short, it is the promoter of the heat current.

In the lesser circulation the current originally started by the genuine idea often goes on continuously and uninterruptedly. It is sometimes accompanied by a feeling of gaiety; sometimes one suddenly experiences a flash of light, which illumines the entire body beyond one's control. This stage is referred to as the spiritual bath. Generally speaking, the achievement of the lesser circulation takes about one hundred days' practice. During this training period the chief task consists in stimulating the heat current by sending the genuine idea to unify heart and kidney. In the Taoist phraseology, this is to compound the mercury from the center of the heart and the lead from the center of the kidney into the elixir of life. To put it in another symbolic fashion, this is the time when the Blue Dragon from the Court of Fire descends to meet the White Tiger from the Abyss of Water. Thus the polarities of *yin* and *yang* are unified and the Golden Flowers bloom. The blooming of the Golden Flowers is due to the union of *yin* and *yang*, and the union of *yin* and *yang*, in turn, is initiated by the concentration on the genuine idea.

After the union of *yin* and *yang* the current rises and falls unceasingly. The pulse is said to stand still and the breathing practically stops. However, through the spine the current ascends suddenly to the top of the head, the higher field of the elixir, where it moves freely by itself. Before the movement of the current ceases, it must be led downward by the idea to the abdomen in the center of the Earth, the regular field of the elixir. This is known as the union of Heaven and Earth, or the grand circulation. In other words, the grand circulation is initiated and also achieved by the genuine idea of concentration.

Scientifically speaking, concentration, or sending one's idea to a certain spot, is to stimulate the nervous system in that region. According to modern neurology, nerve fibers are considered as hollow tubes, normally having a positive electrical charge on the outside and a negative charge on the inside surface. When a stimulus is applied, the charge is reversed in a small region. The outside, which was originally positive, becomes negative, and the inside, formerly negative, becomes positive. This region of reversed polarity, as indicated in Figure 5, then moves along the tube, reversing the charge immediately ahead of it as it moves, and allowing the charge behind the movement to revert to normal. The charge of electricity is called a potential. When a stimulus is applied, we say the resting potential is reversed.

Figure 5 is from the *Fundamentals of Neurology,* by Ernest Gardner. It illustrates the initial change of electrical current in a nerve following stimulation. At *A* we see the fiber as a tube, with the interior exposed. Electrical charges both inside and outside are indicated. At the left end an electric circuit is attached to provide a mild shock. At the right is another circuit to record the results. At *B* the stimulus is applied and the charge begins to reverse, as shown by the arrow

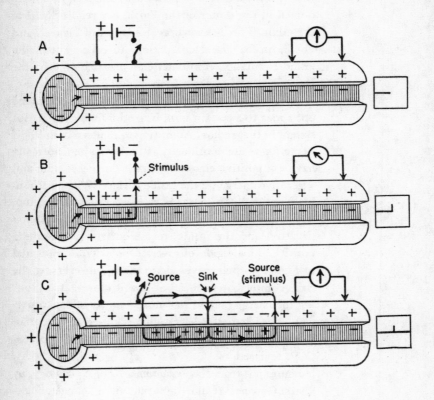

Fig. 5 *The initial change of electrical current in nerve fiber*

near the left end. At *C,* after the charge has been reversed, the nerve impulse is propagated and moves
down the fiber. As the impulse moves, it stimulates the
region ahead of it and thus continues independently
after the original triggering stimulus has ended.

What makes the impulse repeat itself and flow as a
current is simply the artificial stimulus. Thus one
single shock applied to a nerve fiber creates a self-
propagating current and reverses the entire electrical
activity both inside and outside the nerve. This phenomenon initiated by an artificial stimulus is produced
by a psychic stimulus in meditative breathing when
the well-trained practitioner sends the genuine idea to
a certain nerve center. It would be logical to think that
this psychic stimulus applied to the nerve fiber would
also create a self-propagating current and involve a
change of electric charges. Furthermore, when the
practitioner constantly sends the genuine idea to the
nervous system, it moves on unceasingly; a tremendous
change in the electrical charges is effected and the current flow is greatly increased. As the operation in the
serious practitioner goes on month after month, and
year after year, the emergence of "lightning and thunder" within his nervous system will be the natural outcome. Therefore it does not surprise us to learn that
when the Taoist master reaches the highest level of
meditation the "dragon" is revealed and the "thunder"
is heard. Here symbolic language is used to describe
a physical phenomenon. Whether the practitioner's
way of initiating an electric current has the same value
as the method of the electrotherapist would be worthwhile studying. It is obvious that what the Taoist calls
the controlled course is the path of the sympathetic

nerve. When the electric charge works on the sympathetic nerve, the healing of the inner organs will naturally follow, since heart, stomach, and the other inner organs are closely connected with it. Figure 6 also from *Fundamentals of Neurology* by Ernest Gardner shows the relationship between the inner organs and the sympathetic nerve system.

So much for the scientific application of the electric current in the grand circulation. Let us now come back to the actual experience of dragon and thunder of the practitioner. In the fourteenth century there was a certain student who traveled all over South China in his search for *Tao*. One day he saw a very old man meditating in a cave on the top of a mountain. He went up to him and bowed, but the old man ignored his visitor. Inspired by the silence, he immediately sat down opposite the Master. After a while the Master got up to make tea. When the tea was ready, the Master took a cup for himself, put the cup back and resumed his meditation. The visitor then arose and took a cup of tea and put it down as the Master had done. Neither of them uttered a word.

In the evening the Master got up and prepared dinner and ate. The visitor came forward and ate with him. After dinner they both sat again. In the middle of the night the Master got up and took a stroll around the mountain. His guest did likewise; then both returned to their seats. The next day passed in the same manner. They meditated together and shared their simple meals in silence. After seven days the Master spoke, saying, "Sir, where do you come from?" The man replied, "The South." The Master continued, "What makes you come here?" The man said, "To see you."

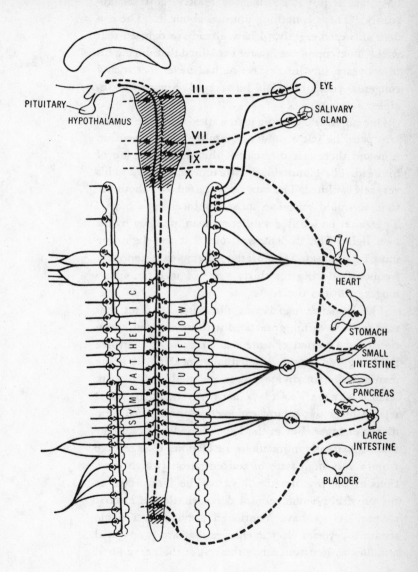

Fig. 6 **The relationship between the inner organs
and the sympathetic nerve system**

"My face is just like this," the Master remarked abruptly. "There is nothing unusual about it." The student answered eagerly, "I have already recognized that well." Thereupon the Master explained that during his thirty years' stay in the cave he had never met such a congenial companion and he accepted him as his disciple.

One night, as the young man walked along the mountain path, he felt a sudden lightning circulate within him and there was the roar of thunder at the top of his head. The mountain, the stream, the world, and his very self vanished. The experience lasted for "about the time it would take five inches of incense to burn." Thereafter he felt like a different man, purified by his own light. The student was told that this lightning must be put aside. The Master, having experienced it frequently during his thirty years of meditation, no longer paid attention to it.

The student's experience illustrates the fact that meditative breathing practiced with utmost concentration over a period of time will bring to the devotee lightning and thunder. Spiritually speaking, it is the manifestation of divine power revealed within man. That is why the Taoist says that when the microcosmic self achieves the utmost quiescence, the heavenly radiance emerges. But in the light of modern neurology these apparently miraculous revelations that emerge from a very high state of concentration (which functions as the psychic stimulus) may be interpreted as the physical phenomenon of depolarization of electric charges. As we have mentioned previously, a single stimulus reverses electric charges that are propagated and flow as a current along the rest of the nerve fiber.

The constant stimulus of concentration on the breath circulation enforces the electric capacity of the current, which circulates over the entire body. Thus spiritual purification could be the depolarization of electric charges in the network of the nervous system. The highest state of concentration is free from any conditioning and entanglement of thought—as demonstrated in our story of the student and the Master.

Having discussed at some length the various circulations and the centers involved in meditative breathing, we should devote a few words to the question of posture, which, I have ascertained, is different in Chinese practice from the imported Indian postures. The earliest Chinese manner of sitting was in kneeling posture, resting the buttocks on the soles of the feet. The ancients, of course, had no chairs but used mats. Of the Emperor Wen in the Han Dynasty (second century) it is reported that when he listened to the philosopher Chia Yi, he became so interested in the discourse that he moved closer and closer to him and didn't even notice that his knees had slid off the mat. We quote Lao Tzu, from the Tao Te Ching: ". . . present Tao to the prince while sitting," by which is meant kneeling, resting one's weight on the soles of the feet. When the practitioner concentrates in this posture on the lower part of his body he, no doubt, will have a feeling as though he were breathing through his heels.

Thus by the word sitting a particular kind of kneeling seems to be meant. In the *Treatise on Kneeling, Sitting and Bowing,* from the works of Chu Hsi (Vol. 68) we read: "The ancients sat by kneeling on both knees and resting back on the upturned soles of the feet." However, to be exact, there are really two ways of kneeling: In "proper kneeling" the two knees touch the ground and the body is held erect. But when the buttocks rest on the soles of the feet the term comfortable sitting is used. In the works of Chu Hsi mentioned above we also find reference to two finely carved sculptures, one of Confucius, the other of Mencius, showing both sitting on their heels. He also speaks of a court in a temple of Confucius when he found a number of beautiful images, all in the sitting-kneeling posture. Then too, when I made a personal study of the writings on the ancient oracle bones, which date back to the Shang Dynasty (about 1400 B.C.) I found pictographs in the ancient manner which show men and women in the same sitting-kneeling posture, with their bodies resting on their heels.

With so much evidence we can probably safely assume that the early Taoist's meditating posture was this ancient way of kneeling, with the body resting on the upturned soles. The heels being the lowest point of contact, they were said to breathe through the heels.

The present-day cross-legged posture is called *Chia fu*. This was introduced from India and originally practiced by the Buddhists. There are two variations of this type of posture. One is called overcoming-the-ghost sitting or *Kang mu*. The practitioner places the toes of the right foot on top of the left thigh and then the toes of the left foot on top of the right thigh. The variant of this posture, called happiness sitting, or *chih chang*, is merely with the position of the legs reversed. This cross-legged way of sitting is certainly not the original Taoist posture.

In the seventeenth century a Neo-Confucianist, Chu Yi-tsun, tells a story about Chen T'uan, the great Taoist master of the fifth century, which may give us a good summary view of the practice of meditative breathing. When Chen T'uan lived in Hua Shan, the sacred mountain in Northwest China, he had the diagram of the ultimateless carved on the cliff where he meditated.

The diagram consisted of several tiers of circles describing the process of meditation. The first tier (the bottom row in the illustration) was a circle labeled, in Lao Tzu's expression, The Gate of the Dark Femininity, which is the Foundation of Heaven and Earth. The next tier is another circle, illustrating the process of compounding *ching* (essence) into *ch'i* (breath), and then into *shên* (spirit). *Ching, ch'i,* and *shên* are the fundamental concepts of meditative breathing, as we have already explained. In other words, this tier shows how the energy from the lowest center of the body is transformed into the circulation of breath and is further transformed into spiritual consciousness. The following, or middle, tier of the diagram consists of the five elements: fire and wood at the left; metal and water at the right; earth in the middle. They symbolize the five movers in the lesser circulation, which ultimately reach the grand circulation. The fourth tier shows the unification of *k'an* and *li* in the form of a circle, which is divided into *yin* and *yang*. The fluctuation of *yin* and *yang* makes the grand circulation through the entire body. Both the five movers in the lesser circulation and *yin* and *yang* in the grand circulation lead to *shên,* or spiritual consciousness. The tier at the top of the drawing shows the compounding of *shên* back to *hsü,* or nonbeing. Thus all things return to *wu chi,* or ultimatelessness. The spiritual consciousness is the ultimate of the individual, and nonbeing is the ultimatelessness.

Fig. 7   Chart of ultimatelessness

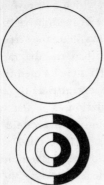

Compounding the spiritual consciousness back to Nonbeing and returning to the ultimatelessness.

To take K'an ☵ unifying with Li ☲

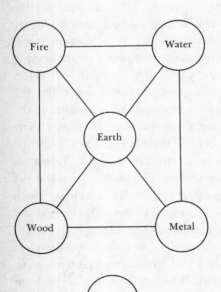

Five breaths assembled at the source

Compounding essence into breath, and compounding breath into spiritual consciousness

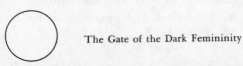

The Gate of the Dark Femininity

In other words, the spiritual consciousness is compounded back to the absolute nonbeing, the origin of all things. This is the basic lesson on which Ch'en T'uan meditated every day.

Philosophically, Chinese meditative breathing is looking into nonbeing, searching for enlightenment. This goal is the same as that recommended by Lao Tzu and Chuang Tzu. They suggested Yoga-like practices as an aid to the attainment of enlightenment, but they did not attempt to work out techniques or build up fanciful symbolisms since they knew that it is only by understanding one's own true nature that enlightenment can come. As Chuang Tzu said: "The fish nets serve to catch fish; let us take the fish and forget the net." The systems built up by later and lesser minds are the fish nets.

As to the value of breathing in the transformation of personality, a well-known German authority wrote me as follows:

. . . I have taken up the practice of meditation myself with the aid of a man who has lived with it for more than thirty years and has proved the value of it by his own development of the inner self. I am convinced that it is the best remedy for neurotic conditions and the sure way to forming the well-adjusted personality of the Real Self. . . . As breathing is a natural action of the body, I believe that the human being who is in harmony with the inner self will breathe in the proper and natural way, just as the man of Tao "breathes deeply from his heels." So all we must do and can do is to help a person to find the way to that inner self, in a wider sense to the union of non-self with self. . . ."

The purpose of meditative breathing is the realization of self, which can be achieved through philosophical understanding without the assistance of breathing exercises. Yoga can be put aside as an unnecessary aid. If it helps the individual in his effort to understand himself and see somewhat more clearly his relationship to the universe around him, then it serves the end of any spiritual exercise: self-realization.

After having gone far into the intricacies of the framework of the Taoist Yoga system, there may be now a need for refreshing ourselves before going on to the next topic, and I believe that the following lines can give us this moment of refreshment:

The mind of man searches outward all day.
The further it reaches,
The more it opposes itself.
Only those who look inward
Can censor their passions,
And cease their thoughts.
Being able to cease their thoughts,
Their minds become tranquil.
To tranquilize their mind is to nourish one's spirit.
To nourish the spirit is to return to Nature.

5 Tranquillity reflected in Chinese poetry

We have discussed the proposition that *Tao,* in its ontological sense, is an inner experience through which man and the universe interfuse as one. This ontological experience is often described as nondifferentiated, nonconceptual, and inexpressible primordial innocence. Chinese poetry in its highest form serves as a means of reflecting this primordial innocence. In Chinese poetry the secret meaning of nature in things is often revealed spontaneously and immediately through the poetic pattern, which emerges from the realm of indeterminacy. When nature's reality stirs the poet's primordial innocence to consciousness, he experiences a pure beauty, which is free and luminous. Jacques Maritain says of this poetic "Innocence": "Creative innocence is the paradise of poetic intuition, the existential state in which poetic intuition can reach full power and liberty." [1] Such pure beauty and spontaneous joy cannot be felt by those who are strangers to the realm in

[1] Jacques Maritain, *Creative Intuition in Art and Poetry,* p. 271.

which man and nature are completely interfused. The famous eleventh-century poem by Ch'eng Hao is a good illustration:

Near the middle of the day, when clouds are thin and the
breeze is light,
I stroll along the river, passing the willows and the bloom-
ing trees.
People of the day do not understand my joy;
They will say that I am loafing like an idle young man.

What is the inner joy of the poet? Why can it not be shared by the "people of the day"? Perhaps I should refer briefly to the story of Confucius and his young disciple, Tsang Tien. Asked to express his most heart-felt wish the latter said that he would want, in the late spring, to go bathing in the river with his companions, to enjoy the breezes and go home singing. The Neo-Confucian commentary considers this an expression of the desire "to rest in the single stream of Heaven and Earth," in which man and all things enjoy themselves. In other words, inner joy is derived from a subjective interfusion with the objective reality of things. The inner joy expressed in the poem of Ch'eng Hao, as well as in the words of Tsang Tien, is an expression of one's ontological experience. Those whose intuition has not reached the highest level cannot understand it. The ordinary man may enjoy the qualitative harmony of forms and colors, but he does not behold the reality within all things. He may see the beauty of appearances, but he fails to perceive the origin of all beauty, which is not beautiful of itself.

On the other hand, the man of *Tao* dives directly into the center of things and establishes an inner rela-tion between nature and man. To him the inner power

of nature is revealed. Nature in turn radiates a new
beauty from her hidden source. This direct contact
with nature produces what the Chinese commentators
call *shên yün,* or spiritual rhythm. It is this spiritual
rhythm vibrating within the poet that gives him joy.
The notion of spiritual rhythm is much emphasized by
Chinese critics as the outcome of an interfusion between the subjectivity of the poet and the objective
reality of things. It is, in fact, an invisible interplay between two poles. The sphere of this deep-seated subjective feeling between two poles is *ching chiai;* it is
the inner realm of the poet within which the spiritual
rhythm moves. Every one of us has an inner structure
of his own. With each of us it is unique. We all absorb
different elements from the objective world and the
content and horizon of our inner realm vary accord-
ingly. For the ordinary man this content is limited to
differentiation of forms and his horizon cannot exceed
the limitations of his experiences. The inner realm of
the poet, his *ching chiai,* has, so to speak, no visible content; therefore his horizon has no limits. In his realm
the mind acts freely and spontaneously without discursive restrictions. It moves of itself and the poet may
not even be conscious of it. It is from this realm of the
unconscious that the pattern of his poetry emerges into
consciousness. The following ancient Chinese song
may serve to illustrate this:

As soon as the sun rises
We start to work.
As soon as the sun sets
We take our rest.
We dig the well
And we drink.

We till the land
And we eat—
What has the power of Ti[2] to do with us?

This man's life—working, resting, eating, drinking
—is as innocently real as the moonlight and the falling
rain. His mind is free from all traces of man-made
restrictions and limitations. Thus there is no way of de-
termining the horizon of his inner realm. He is in harmony with all his surroundings. There exists no boundary between self and nonself. In the barest essentials
of the simple life there is a residue of spiritual power,
which is free from conceit and egotism. The innocent
and the spiritual aspects, though they appear to be
different, are in reality one and the same. The minds
of both the innocent and the spiritual man are free
from any trace of conflict, free from entanglements of
artificiality.

In the last chapter of the works of Chuang Tzu we
find a description of the "complete man," the man who
identifies with both the natural and the spiritual aspects of existence:

The man who is not divorced from the great source is
the natural man. The man who is not divorced from the essence is the spiritual man.

The commentator of this passage says that although
we speak variously of the natural man and the spiritual
man he is actually one, the complete man. The inner
realm of the complete man is free from obstructions
and not distorted or confused by external things. He
identifies with the Universe and interfuses with all
things. He is not the ego-self but the unlimited non-

[2] *Ti* may denote the god, or the imperial power.

ego-self. This self sometimes manifests itself as primordial innocence, sometimes as transcendental spirituality. Both are fundamental to poetic expression.

In the works of the great Chinese poets both of these aspects are manifested. Li P'o (701-762), in a poem entitled "Thoughts in the Quiet Night," naïvely sings:

In front of my bed the moonlight shone.
For a moment I took it for frost on the floor.
When I lifted my head, I saw that it was the moon.
When I bent my head, I dreamt of my far-away home.

These charming lines of Li P'o reflect his poetic innocence as immediately as the moonlight on the floor. In another poem he expresses his transcendental joy that he experienced in the solitude of the mountains:

You ask me why I stay in these blue mountains.
I smile but I do not answer.
O, my mind is at ease!
Peach blossoms and flowing streams pass without a trace.
How different from the mundane world!

Whenever the Chinese poet has reached this tranquil depth he reflects his original simplicity or reveals his inexhaustible inner joy. Primordial innocence and luminous joy are two aspects of the one ontological experience. According to Taoist theory, this ontological experience is intuitive self-awareness, which is different from discursive thinking. It is the uncarved block, formless, soundless, colorless—yet latent in it are all forms, all sounds, and all colors. From this state of non-being, which is intangible and undefinable, all that is tangible and definable is produced. The creative process of the universe is also the creative process of the poet, who has transformed his ego into self and thus has become part of the universe.

Western critics also hold the view that poetic experience in the highest sense is invisible, intangible, unknowable. The idea of the synthesis of poetic and ontological experience has been expounded at length by Martin Heidegger:

> The poet knows that, in calling the discovery "the reserved," he is saying something which the ordinary understanding will struggle against. . . . That is why the poet, almost as soon as he has spoken the line about the mystery of the reserving proximity, has to descend to the phrase: "Foolish is my speech." But nevertheless he is speaking. The poet must speak, for "It is joy." . . . The writing of poetry is not primarily a cause of joy to the poet, rather the writing of poetry is joy, is serenification, because it is in writing that the principal return home consists. . . . To write poetry means to exist in that joy, which preserves in words the mystery of proximity to the Most Joyous.[3]

Heidegger further maintains:

> The Serene preserves and holds everything in tranquility and wholeness. . . . It is the holy. For the poet, the "Highest" and the "holy" are one and the same; the Serene. As the origin of all that is joyous it remains the Most Joyous. Here there occurs the pure serenification.[4]

It is this pure serenification that constitutes the highest achievement of Chinese poets, to whom ontological and poetic experience are one.

The intricacy of the poetic process is fundamentally the reflection of objective reality, and this reflection can only take place successfully when the poet obtains

[3] Martin Heidegger, *Existence and Being*, pp. 280-281, Henry Regnery, 1949.
[4] *Ibid.*, p. 271.

the "pure serenification" and experiences "the mystery of proximity to the Most Joyous." It is the poet's mission to make the reader participate in his inner experience and enter the realm of pure serenification. In other words, the reader is carried into the rhythmic flux and is brought to the depth of original indeterminacy from which the poetic pattern emerges. The reader is directly confronted with the objective reality which the poet originally faced. The subjectivity of the reader and the objective reality in the poem interfuse without obstruction and distortion from the interference of the poet. This is what Chinese critics call the principle of directness. Wang Kuo-wei in his work entitled *Criticism of Poetry in the Mundane World* states:

> The poems written by T'ao Ch'ien (373-427) and Hsieh Ling-yun (385-433) give you the impression of directness. The poems by Li Yen-nien sometimes not. . . .
> The idea of directness can be illustrated by the following lines: "Around the pond April grass is growing," or "Under the beam the swallows' nest is empty, from it the clay is dropping." The effectiveness of these lines is brought about by the subtlety of directness.

The pond growing with April grass, the deserted nest of the swallows, the clay falling, all describe the situation with which the poet was confronted. The situation is brought to the reader without comment from the poet. When the actual situation is presented to the reader, with the poet's own interpretation unexpressed, the reader is free to react to it. The objective reality of the poem speaks directly to the innermost being of the reader. There is no attempt to impose any specific ideas upon the reader's conscious mind. Rather, his mind is allowed to react freely and spontaneously.

This idea of establishing immediacy between the reader and the poem is described in the following lines by Jacques Maritain:

Such poems are condensed, the expression is purely restricted to the essentials, any discursive or oratorial development and liaison has been replaced by allusive streaks. But they are clear poems. . . . the intelligible sense, although still explicit, is, as it were, not circumscribed, I would say, open.[5]

To do away with the intermediary of expressed concepts means to eliminate possible distortion by the subjectivity of the poet. This is the directness of which the Chinese critic speaks. This directness makes the things in the poem be themselves. Existence itself is poetical. The poetry is merely an expression of such existence. Chinese poets penetrate into the source of things and reveal their true nature. As Archibald MacLeish would say, "A poem should not mean, but be!" The best works of Chinese poetry do not "mean"; they "are." The spiritual rhythm emerges from the objective reality, which appears no more a mere visual description.

In Spring when all the flowers are in bloom,
The evening river appears smooth and motionless.
Suddenly the tidewater comes with the reflection
*   of glittering stars;*
The ebbing waves carry away the image of the moon.
                              Yang Kwang

In quiescence I hear the cinnamon blossoms fall.
When the night has come, the Spring mountains are silent.

[5] *Op. cit.,* p. 196.

Suddenly the moon appears from behind the clouds
   and startles the young birds;
By the mountain stream they chirp and chirp.

                          Wang Wei (701-761)

The above poems have a quality of self-sustaining reality. Their action in nonaction awakens an inner reality and the reader is carried along with it. It is not through logical conceptualization that the poem and the reader are brought together but through the spiritual rhythm flowing back and forth between the objective reality of the picture and the subjective reality of the beholder. The inexpressible flux between the two poles is not subject to the artificiality of external rules. When the poet is free from artificiality he will not only reflect pure objective reality, he will also be able to reflect spontaneously his inner joy without distortion and limitations from the ego-consciousness. He is purposeless and fearless as the flowing stream and the shining moon. Since the poet is serene he simply reflects what happens to his mind.

In Spring I was soundly asleep;
Hardly did I notice the break of the day.
Everywhere I heard the birds singing.
Last night there was the noise of storm and rain;
I wonder how many blossoms have blown away.

                  Meng Hao-jan (689-740)

Since the days of my middle life
I was deeply devoted to Tao.
Recently I came to live
In the mountain of Chung-nan.
Oftentimes—with joy in my heart—
Alone, I roam here and there.
It is a wonderful thing

That I am aware of myself.
When the streamlet ends my trip
I settle down and catch
The moment of rising mists.
Now and then I meet
A furrowed dweller of the woods.
We chat and laugh;
Never do we want to go home.

Wang Wei

The simplicity and naturalness reflected in the above poems lead the reader to the serene realm of the poet. The reader is made to experience what the poet originally experienced from the actual situation. He faces directly the objective reality in the poem and shares the ontological experience of the poet. The directness both of the pure objective presentation and the poet's inner joy are derived from his self, which affects the self of the reader, though he may not be aware of it.

Wang Kuo-wei speaks of two categories of the poet's inner world: the inner world of the nonego-self and the inner world of the ego-form self. When the poet lives in the realm of the nonego-self he sees things as they actually are; he does not distort their actuality. Wang Kuo-wei uses the following lines as an illustration:

The wintry ripples in the lake gently move away;
White seagulls lightly swoop down.

In these lines the poet merely brings out the objective reality grasped by him in a moment when his nonego-self is revealed. The great self reflects things, but does not change them. From the realm of the ego-form-self, Wang Kuo-wei maintains, the poet projects his subjective feelings to the objective actuality,

thereby changing the reality of things. He gives us the
following illustration:

With tears in my eyes I ask the flowers to share my sorrow.
Alas! the flowers all remain silent!
And the scattered petals blow away to the swing.[6]

The poet personifies the flowers by projecting his
own feelings on them. Silence is the actuality of the
flowers and the drifting of the petals is aimless and
emotionless. However, by the poet's brush the silence
of the flowers and the floating petals becomes the poet's
subjective feeling of unwillingness to share his grief.
This type of poetry seems to be what T. S. Eliot calls
"the negative aspect of poetic experience." He says:

It seems that at these moments which are characterized
by the sudden lifting of the burden of anxiety and fear
which presses upon our daily life so steadily. . . . What
happens is something negative, that is to say, "not inspiration" as we commonly think. . . . Some obstruction is
momentarily whisked away. The accompanying feeling is
less like what we know as positive pleasure, than a sudden
relief from an intolerable burden.[7]

When the Chinese poet has an emotional conflict,
which causes inner tension, he is oftentimes relieved
after his drinking and poem-making. The vibration of
his inner melody indicates the intensity of his conflict.
The following lines testify to the inner melody of an
excessive anxiety:

Withered vine,
Rotten tree,
Dark crow,

[6] Swing, a recreation apparatus for girls, used in early days.
[7] T. S. Eliot, *The Use of Poetry and the Use of Criticism*, p. 137.

Little bridge,
Running stream,
Homestead,
Worn-out road,
Western wind,
Lean horse,
The sun is setting in the west;
The broken-hearted man is at the end of the earth.

This poem was written by Ma Chih-yuan of the thirteenth century, who projects his own feelings to color the objects he describes. The feelings aroused in the poet may not be shared by others, even though confronted with the very same situation. In a recent paper Herbert Read gives his approval to the findings of Maud Bodkin in *Archetypal Patterns in Poetry:*

The self which is asserted is magnified by that same collective force to which finally submission is made; and from the tension of two impulses and their reaction upon each other, under conditions of poetic exaltation, the distinctive tragic attitude and emotion appear to arise.

The poetic exaltation of the broken-hearted man indicates the exaggerated self-assertion of the poet which modifies all the objects in the poem. This kind of poetry is written to release the excessive tension of the ego-centered self. The objects in the poem are colored by emotions from the poet's distorted inner world.

Such poetry will have the reader's attention as well as his sympathy. However, it can merely reach his limited ego-centered realm; it cannot penetrate the primordial source from which the great compassion springs. When the great compassion is stirred, its power breaks down all limiting barriers of the ego-self. The self, expanding beyond itself, becomes the self of others. This fusion reveals the realm of the universal great self, which, according to the Taoists, is the real self. The great Chinese poet, Tu Fu (712-770), who dwelt in the realm of the real self, is honored as the Sage Poet. His best poetry reflects the great compassion and therefore touches the hidden depth of the hearts of men. The following poem, which has been considered one of his masterpieces, is a good illustration:

When it was dark, I reached the village of Shih-hao.
Late at night an officer came to recruit men.
The old man in the house climbed over the wall and fled.
The old woman opened the door.
How the angry officer was raging!
How bitterly the woman was crying!
I heard what the old woman said:
"I had three sons for the defense of the City of Yeh.
Only one of them sent me a letter.
The other two boys were killed in the battle.
The one who remained may not live long.
The dead are gone forever.
There are no more men in the house
Except my grandson who is still fed on milk.
Because of him his mother stays with us.
However, she has no whole skirt to go out.
Although I am old and have no strength,
Let me go with you, officer,
To immediately answer the urgent call from Ho-yang.
At least I can do some cooking for the soldiers."
Later in the night their conversation stopped.
What I heard was something like sobbing.
At daybreak I started out again on my journey.
I could only say "Good-bye" to the old man.

In this poem Tu Fu simply presents objective actuality to which the readers will react in the same way—they all will share the poet's great sympathy. Not one word is expressed on morality or sympathy, yet from the purely objective picture painted by the poet shines the great compassion. It is through this primordial powerful compassion that he dissolves his self into the selves of others and grasps the secret of poetic creativity, which places his works far beyond the reach of lesser poets. Western critics have also recognized the relationship between great poetry and self-realization. For instance Jacques Maritain says:

> The creative self of the artist is his person as person . . . not his person as material individual or as self-centered ego. And the first obligation imposed on the poet is to consent to be brought back to the hidden place near the center of the soul, where this totality exists in the state of a creative source.[8]

In the process of creation there exists no ego-self. The poetic work is brought forth from the primordial source of the great self. Its achievement is beyond artificial and measurable effort; it expands from the finite to the infinite, from the limited to the limitless.

The dynamic forces in great poetry often break the barriers of space and time and become "indubitable magic" or *shên yün,* as the Chinese put it. This power of the creative self is illustrated in Chu Hsi's following poem:

The wide pond expands like a mirror,
The heavenly light and cloud shadows play upon it.
How does such clarity occur?
It is because it contains the living stream from the Foun
    tain.

To understand further this Fountain or primordial source we may read another poem by Chu Hsi:

[8] *Op. cit.,* p. 106.

We study the Changes (I Ching) after the lines
  have been put together.
Why should we not set our minds on that which was
  before any line was drawn?
When we understand that Two Forms have originated
  from the Ultimate
We can safely say that we can cease to study the
  I Ching.

The ultimate in this poem is identical with the primordial source in the first poem. And the constant changes of forms and their divisions derived from the ultimate are the living stream. According to Chou Tun-yi the ultimate is also the ultimateless. To use the Taoist expression, "Being is produced from Nonbeing." All energies and possibilities are derived from nonbeing and rejuvenated by it. The importance of nonbeing, or the void, is particularly emphasized in the *Literary Mind and the Carving of the Dragons* where we read:

Void and Quietude are primarily essentials in the cultivation of literary thought, because they rejuvenate the internal organs and refresh the spirit.

The idea of the void is also emphasized in Lu Chi's *Wen Fu* or *The Art of Letters*, which has been translated by E. R. Hughes. We read:

Oblivious to all sights, oblivious to all sounds, both sunk in thought and questioning abroad. His spirit was away on a wild gallop to the Eight Poles, his mind thousands of cubits beneath the sod. Then he reached to this point: the dawn of his mood grew brighter and so more defined, the objects of his attention lighted up and came jostling forward.

. . . He was taxing Non-Being to produce Being, calling to Silence, importuning for an answer.[9]

Most of the great Chinese poets were well trained in the art of meditation. And the special quality of their poems is called *San Mei,* or *samadhi.* This quality, peculiar to their works, is the essence brought forth from meditation, through which the universal self is achieved and from which the spiritual rhythm issues forth. The Chinese poet is expected to cultivate himself to such a state as described by a Zen Buddhist in the following lines:

Through Quiescence and Void confusion is dissolved,
As the white clouds break up when they reach a wintry cliff.
Spiritual light dispels the darkness,
As the moonlight follows the path of the night vessel.

Creative activity in the highest sense has its origin in nonbeing, or the void. The great Chinese poets who, by self-cultivation and meditation, penetrated to the void, have produced truly great works. They owe a great debt to the ancient Taoists who taught that the contemplation of the utmost in quietude will lead to the hidden recesses of creative power and that it is from this realm that beauty is manifested to the objective world. A high level of self-cultivation gives them that absolute freedom and serenity which makes for natural reflection, without preconceptions and distortions. Here I would like to quote a series of poems by various poets on the subject of meditation itself:

I go to sleep as spontaneously as the birds go back
*   to the forest.*

[9] Lu Chi, A.D., 261-303, *The Art of Letters,* translated by E. R. Hughes, pp. 96-98.

*During the day my mind is as carefree as that of the
     begging monk.
My life is like the crane's who cries a few times
     under the pine tree.
And like the silent light from the lamp in the
     bamboo grove.
In the middle of the night I sit with legs crossed.
I do not even answer the call from my daughter or
     my wife.*

                                   P'o Chü-i (772-846)

*There is a meditative terrace left by the ancient
     Master Chi.
It is so high that it is always covered with white clouds.
Should the woodcutter see it, he would not recognize it;
The mountain monks, however, were glad to find it.
They thought it would interest me and took me there to
     see it.
Throughout the night dew drops fall leisurely from the
     bamboos;
During the day pure breezes blow from the pine grove.
Meditation is what I used to do as the first thing;
The terrace of Master Chi inspires me even more.*

                                        Meng Hao-jan

*Lately I became aware of the meaning of Quietude.
Day after day I stayed away from the multitude.
I cleaned my cottage and prepared it for the visit of a monk
Who came to me from the distant mountains.
He descended from the cloud-hidden peaks
To see me in my thatched house.
Sitting in the grass we shared the resin of the pine.
Burning incense we read the sutras of Tao.
When the day was over we lighted our lamp.
The temple bells announced the beginning of the evening.
Suddenly I realized that Quietude is indeed Joy,
And I felt that my life has abundant leisure.*

                                        Wang Wei

*To return to the Heavenly mind is to return to No-mind.
When the mind becomes No-mind it is nowhere to be
     found.*

If you say that No-mind is nothing,
How can you then say:
"From the Abysmal Water is produced the Golden Elixir."

　　　　　　　Shao K'ang-chi (1011-1077)

The clouds emerge from the Mountain of Chung
And then return to the Mountain of Chung.
I would like to ask the dweller in this mountain,
"Where are the clouds now?"
Clouds emerge from No-mind
And then return to No-mind.
No-mind is nowhere to be found.
We need not seek the home of No-mind.

　　　　　　　Wang An-shih (1068-1076)

When the moon rises in the Heart of Heaven
And a light breeze touches the mirror-like face
　　of the lake,
That is indeed a moment of pure joy.
But few are they who are aware of it.

　　　　　　　Anon.

Purity and joy are the fruits of meditation. For the Chinese poets they are fundamental to poetic creativity. The higher their level of self-cultivation, the better their poetry. As Yen Yü, the famous twelfth-century poetry critic, says:

Generally speaking, the Way of Buddhism lies on enlightenment. The way of poetry also lies on enlightenment. Meng Hao-yen's academic achievement is far below that of Han Yü (769-824). Meng's poetry is much better than that of Han Yü. The reason for this is that Meng has achieved enlightenment, but Han has not.

Before a poet is enlightened he sees flowers as flowers, and willows as willows. But when he is enlightened, although he still sees flowers as flowers and willows as willows, he is now aware of the spiritual rhythm within the flowers and the willows. As the Zen Buddhist sings:

When the wild birds sing their melodies from the tops of
    the trees,
They carry the thoughts of the Patriarch.
When the mountain flowers are blooming, the genuine
    meaning of Tao
Comes along with their fragrance.

Most Confucianists write poetry. But those who have achieved enlightenment always give us good verse. Wang Yang-ming (1472-1529), who was enlightened, states:

Profound quietude delivered me to the transparent moon-
    light.
After enlightenment one understands that the Six Classics
    contain not even a word.

Some of his works were selected by Wang Wen-lu of the sixteenth century, who claims that his poems have the same quality of directness and lucidity as those of the Tang poets. Wang Wen-lu quotes a few lines as an illustration:

In the night the bells of the mountain temple
Are swung by the wind from the pines.
From my bed of stone by the wintry lamp
I can hear the flowering rain of Buddha.

The mists rise up to the mountain peaks;
They are submerging the temple.
Through the scattered trees of the forest
I see the river down in the valley.

The following two poems may serve as a further illustration:

Grotesque rocks form a thousand hollows;
The ancient pines bear shattered limbs.
The pure breeze sweeps the mountain cavern;
This is the time for my return.

No one escapes the summer heat among men.
All breezes blow deep in the mountain.
Three days I sat beside the lake.
Suddenly I saw a flame light up
In the green tree on the cliff.

The quality of directness and purity in poetry, strongly emphasized by Chinese critics, is the immediate reflection from the poet's mind; it is devotion to quietude that leads to the mind of no-mind. When the poet has achieved the mind of no-mind, his subjectivity interfuses with the objective reality of things. "Things are grasped in the Self and the Self is grasped in Things." When there is this perfect interfusion, subjectivity and objectivity awaken in a single flash. This spontaneous outburst of poetic intuition is rooted in ontological intuition and manifested in the poetic work, which is full of life and movement, not hampered by any artificiality. Maritain says:

Poetic intuition . . . only wants to manifest the inwardness of the poet, together with the things which resound in it—and if poetic intuition is really expressed it will inevitably be expressed in beauty even without meaning it.

He also points out that such inevitable expression of beauty ". . . cannot be attained except as in a mirror, and is still escaping our grasp, and Poetry is not directed to any definite end." [10]

The Chinese critics use various metaphors to de-

[10] *Op. cit.,* p. 132.

scribe this immediate flash, such as "the image of blossoms in a mirror," "the moon transparent in the water," or, as the Zen Buddhists say, "the goat leaves no trace when hanging by her horns from the tree." This natural flash that leaves no trace is revealed in the following poems:

By the western cliff an old fisherman sleeps
* through the night.*
At dawn he draws water from the Hsiang River
* and makes a bamboo fire.*
Mists melt away, the sun rises, no man has yet appeared.
The oar rasps; suddenly the mountain and
* the river are green.*
Sailing in the middle of the stream, he gazes back toward
* the infinite sky.*
From the cliffs the clouds follow him without intention.
Liu Chung-yuan (773-819)

In the deep bamboo forest I sit alone.
Loudly I sing and tune my lute.
The forest is so thick that no one knows about it.
Only the bright moon comes to shine upon me.
Wang Wei

By the screen, on my bamboo couch, with a stone for
* my pillow,*
I dozed, and my book fell from my weary hand.
When I woke up, I was full of joy and smiled silently.
Suddenly, from the river, fragments of melodies came
* over from the fisherman's flute.*
Ts'ai Ch'o

Spring breezes sweep the green meadows.
Rains have stopped, but from the bamboo leaves
* water still drips.*
Suddenly a white bird appears on the scene.
He breaks the green universe of the mountain slope.
P'o Yü-ch'ien

In each of the above poems we have a clear presentation of the poetic situation without interference from the poet's ego. Therefore an immediate contact is established between the situation that the poet faced and the reader. The directness in the poems is due to the pure reflection of the poet's experience. The last line of each of the poems, especially, reveals the free movment of the absolute moment. It is the sudden awakening of objective reality through a flash of the subjective consciousness. Its manifestation is the poetic work. From the poetic work we are often led back to the source of creativity and immediately share in the ontological experience. When P'o Yu-ch'ien was asked about immortality he answered in the following words: "When someone asks me about the ways of immortality, I speak no word, but silently point to the falling blossoms." The ontological experience is inexpressible. P'o Yu-ch'ien simply points to the falling blossoms without uttering a word. In this way he reveals the highest truth, which is called first principle by the Buddhists. This highest truth or first principle is also accomplished by T'ao Ch'ien in the following poem, which was discussed in the chapter on Sympathy:

To build a house in the world of man
And not to hear the noise of horse and carriage,
How can this be done?—
When the mind is detached, the place is quiet.
I gather chrysanthemums under the eastern hedgerow
And silently gaze at the southern mountains.
The mountain air is beautiful in the sunset,
And the birds flocking together return home.
In all these things there is a real meaning,
Yet when I want to express it, I become lost in no-words.

In this poem we can see the fluctuation from the primordial source of the poet's mind to the manifestation of objective reality and from objective reality back again to the primordial source. Psychologically speaking, there is a free movement from the depth of the unconscious, which carries images and conceptions to the conscious. When images and conceptions have been dissolved in the process of blending subjectivity with objectivity, our poet returns to the depth of the unconscious. It is in this way that he identifies his poetic experience with ontological experience and leads the reader to the ground of all beauty.

According to Wang An-shih, the extreme beauty of T'ao Ch'ien's poems cannot be equaled by any other works because no poet had ever given so much of his inner experience in his works. T'ao Ch'ien's achievement is due to self-cultivation rather than to the refinement of artificial techniques. T'ao Ch'ien was not only greatly honored as a poet, but he was also held in high esteem on account of his inner qualities. He was a good friend of Hui Yuan, the great fourth-century Buddhist, who broke the rules of the temple to entertain him with wine. Hui Yuan had lived in the Mountain Lu for thirty years and had never left it even to go beyond the Tiger Brook. But when he saw his guest T'ao Ch'ien off one day, he did not realize that he had gone one hundred paces beyond the Tiger Brook until he heard a tiger roar.

Most Chinese critics emphasize the purity and simplicity of T'ao Ch'ien. But there is another important aspect to be considered: the unrestrained, vigorous, and virile feeling, which is the natural reflection of his mirror-like mind. This aspect has not often been recognized by Chinese critics, but Chu Hsi points out that—

. . . although the poetry of Yuan-ming (T'ao Ch'ien) is mostly conceived of as pure and light, he revealed his primordial Self in an unrestrained and vigorous manner in his "Song for Ching K'o." How can a man be said to be limited to "purity and simplicity" when on other occasions he expresses himself in such strong, heroic words.

To prove this point, let us quote these words:

Prince Tan of Yen knew well how to treat a brave man.
One day he vowed to give a lesson to the tyrant-state of Chin.
He set out to gather hundreds of brave men of Yin.
At the end of the year he found the hero Ching K'o.
Ching K'o understood that "a man of honor must die for the one who appreciates him."
He decided to take up his sword and leave the capital.
Gloriously he was seen off.
His white horse was neighing while trotting on the highway.
His angry hair pointed up to his helmet,
Its band, waving in the wind, betrayed his fierce spirit.
On reaching the bank of the river, he drank with all the heroes,
Who had gathered around him to bid him good-bye.
The hero Chien Li played the lute in a sad tone;
Sung-Yi sang in a loud lamenting voice.
A melancholy breeze swept by quietly,
And cold ripples moved over the river.
The sorrowful notes moved everyone to tears,
But the martial music stirred the heart of the hero Ching K'o.
He knew that once you have left, you never return.
All that is left behind is a name for the generations to come.

He immediately mounted the chariot, not looking back
for a moment.
He covered ten thousand miles, not counting difficulties
and hardships;
He went around ten thousand cities;
Then—swiftly he entered the court of Chin.
The map of Yen was presented.
It was unrolled until the dagger was exposed.
How the tyrant prince trembled!
Woe! the dagger's skill failed him;
The heroic deed was not accomplished.
The man is gone forever,
But his spirit has remained with us for a thousand years.[12]

In this poem the poet gives us a description of heroic deeds in a purely objective manner. The vitality and vigor permeating the lines do not come from the ego-self but from the hidden power of the limitless nonego self. When this power remains in nonaction, we have serenity but, when in action, we have manifestations of various kinds, such as Tu Fu's loyalty to his nation, or P'o Chu-yi's love for the people, or T'ao Ch'ien's astounding feats of valor as in the poem of Ching K'o which we have just discussed.

The common assumption that the Chinese poet who has reached serenity is limited to conveying the purity of nature is only partially correct. Of course the poet often reveals the secret meanings of nature in the singing of birds, the movement of the bamboo, or in the fragrance of the spring blossoms. But he never loses sight of common worldly activities. When the people

[12] Ching K'o, under the pretense of surrendering the territory of Yen, carried with him a map of his state to present to the Prince of Chin. In the rolled-up map a dagger was concealed. When he unrolled the map in front of the prince the dagger was exposed. He seized it and stabbed the tyrant ruler, but he merely wounded him, thus failing in his attempt to assassinate him. Ching K'o was killed on the spot.

cry, he cries with them; when they laugh, he laughs with them. When the people suffer an injustice, he arouses public sympathy; when he hears of great deeds, he praises the man, setting him up as a model for generations to come. By the poet's magic the most ordinary happenings become completely transformed. He lifts them out of their dull atmosphere, imbuing them with a spiritual content. One man's experience becomes the experience of all. The particular becomes the universal. This magnificent transformation cannot be expected from mere mechanical skill. It is only when the poet has reached serenity that he is able to give a mirror-like reflection of all of human experience.

In Chinese poetry there are sensuous forms of words and images as well as various rhythmic patterns. Chinese characters are meaningful images and symbols, yet such individual characters can limit the poet in expressing his ideas and feelings. But when the poet has an ontological experience, his intuition will be so powerful that it will break down all barriers. Symbols, images, rhythmical perfection, although carefully studied by certain schools, such as the one called the Kiang-hsi School, headed by Huang Shan-ku (1045-1105), has never been considered as of primary importance by the great poets, since refinement of form has often ended in triviality. The main concern of the great Chinese poet has always been to reach the state of inner serenity, as he realizes that only the enlightened man produces great and lasting works. The mirror-like mind is not necessarily the product of gradual meditation; it can also be the product of a sudden awakening of the mind. In the Zen literature we find many instances of such experiences. As soon as the Zenist is enlightened, a poem, manifesting his experience, flows from his lips. Zen itself is inexpressible, as we know, but the man who has found Zen by the way of sudden enlightenment wishes to reflect his joyous experience. He tells us how enlightenment came to him and how his attitude toward the world has changed as a result of his experience. The following are examples:

Neither by words nor by the patriarch;
Neither by colors nor by sound was I enlightened.
But, at midnight, when I blew out the candle and went to
*   bed,*
Suddenly, within myself, I reached the dawn.

For about thirty years I wandered,
Searching for the real Tao everywhere.
How many times did I see the trees
Grow new branches and watch the old leaves fall.
But at this moment, seeing the peach blossoms,
I am suddenly enlightened and have no more doubts.

There is nothing so close as the teaching of "Suchness."
A grain of sand contains all land and sea.
When we have found the truth
There is no single man in the Great Earth.

Although in the strict sense these Zenists are not poets, their verse flows forth spontaneously as water from a fountain. It is to this deep underlying fountain that the Chinese literary critic Liu Hsieh refers in the following passage:

Spiritual action is transmitted by symbols in which feelings and changes are conceived. The knowledge of things is learned through their appearances, but the awareness of reality is reflected in the heart.[13]

[13] *Op. cit.*, Chapter XXVI, "Spiritual Thought."

The commentator Wêng Fang-kang has spoken of reality in this way:

Those who have achieved an understanding of reality can describe the wonder of things, but those who are ignorant of reality miss the essence of things.

He continues:

He who possesses an understanding of reality can reach the subtlety of things in accordance with their natural spontaneity. His mind interfuses and his spirit becomes one with things. Silently he comes into accord with their action and non-action. When he reaches this invisible fountain, he can express it in all forms in which both appearances and essence move and vibrate. Hence, the forms are given the breath of life and move with their own rhythm.

When we examine the works of T'ao Ch'ien, Wang Wei, Li P'o, Meng Hao-yen, P'o Chü-i and many others, we find that their works have distinct characteristics and each of them makes his own contribution to the beauty of poetry. As Chu Hsi says in his famous lines:

If we simply recognize the face of the eastern wind
Each of the thousand flowers, in red or purple, is Spring.

The face of the eastern wind indicates the ground, the realm of nondifferentiation, or the intrinsic indeterminacy of the poet's mind. Our inner awareness of this realm of indeterminacy is described by Lao Tzu as "invisible, inaudible, unfathomable." He says:

It is impossible to define.
So again it turns back into Non-Being.

Thus it is called the form of the formless,
And the image of the imageless (Chapter XVII).

It is this formless, imageless, and undefinable to which Herbert Read refers when he discusses "Poetic Consciousness and Creative Experience":

> The poem is a sensuous unity, a totality of utterance, and meaningful as unity or totality. To break it down into image and idea is to ignore the fact that there are no internal sutures, no possibility of separating image from image, image from idea, either from the language in which they are expressed.
> Do we then end with a mystery, and a veto on psychological attempts to explain it? Not exactly. We end with the reality of being or existence, and the experience of poetry is a proof of its intrinsic originality, or its ceaseless novelty, of its impredictable form . . . The immediate object of the poetic experience refuses to be identified: It is infinite and eternal, formless and uninformed.[14]

This infinite, formless, and uninformed experience is the highest achievement of poetry in which poetic intuition identifies with ontological experience, the attainment of *Tao*. Along with the revelation of *Tao* comes the inner joy which is beyond the comprehension of ordinary man as Ch'eng Hao stated in his poem which was discussed in the beginning of this chapter. What was considered the ground of poetry by the ancients of the Eastern world is also conceived of as fundamental to the creativity of modern poetry and art.

Let us quote again from Herbert Read:

> The sense of delight is, I think, the sense of illumination, of revelation, what Maritain calls specifically "the

[14] Herbert Read, "Poetic Consciousness and Creative Experience," *Eranos Jahrbuch,* XXV, 1956, pp. 383-384.

poetic sense," a meaning which is immanent in the object which is a poem or consubstantial with it." [15]

In the foregoing I have tried to trace the "meaning" immanent in Chinese poetry, now I shall proceed to do the same in the field of Chinese painting.

[15] *Ibid.*

6 Tranquillity reflected in Chinese painting

○   In the course of analyzing Chinese poetry we found that whenever a poet identified his personal poetic experience with the ontological experience he produced works of the highest quality. Such works, which are reflections from the center of the poet's being, open our hearts when we chant their rhymes.

    Similarly, we find that the great masters of painting make their contributions only when they have had such ontological experience and dwell in a state of inner serenity. Like the poet, the artist then gives us pure reflections of nature's "untouched primacy." Since the inner serenity of the poet and the painter are the same in their essence, it is not surprising that we are often enchanted with the poetic atmosphere of a painting and, on the other hand, struck by the beauty of a scene depicted in a poem. The following incidents from the lives of great Chinese poet-artists will substantiate our contention that poetry and painting spring from a common inner source.

Yen Chen-ching of the eighth century, famous for his calligraphy, sent five poems of his creation to a friend named Chang Chih-ho, one of the three great Taoist masters of painting,[1] who was generally known by his pen name, Fisherman of Mists and Ripples. The subtle beauty of these poems so moved Chang that he immediately painted the scenes described in them. Human figures, fishing boats, mists and ripples, wind and moon, were all imbued with the exquisite subtlety characteristic of the poems. The transference of an inner experience which, in this instance, took place between contemporaries, can also occur between individuals living centuries apart, as is illustrated in the following episode.

The master, Shih T'ao[2] *(1641-c. 1717)* was inspired by a poet who had lived centuries before him, Su Tung-p'o (1036-1101). It so happened that one day when a heavy snowstorm was raging outside his cottage, Shih T'ao was suddenly moved to seize his brush and execute a series of drawings that were transpositions of Su Tung-p'o's twelve poems describing the scenery at the various seasons of the year. This is how Shih T'ao recounted the incident:

This album had been on my desk for about a year and never once did I touch it. One day, when a snow storm was blowing outside, I thought of Su Tung-p'o's poems describing twelve scenes and became so inspired that I took up my brush and started painting each of the scenes in the poems. At the top of each picture I copied the original

[1] The other two, according to Chinese critics: Mi Fei (1051-1107) and Ni Tsan (1301-1374).

[2] Shih T'ao is a pen name, meaning Stone Wave. His Buddhist name is Tao-chi; he was a member of the royal line of the Ming Dynasty (1368-1644), originally known as Chu Yu-chi. He turned monk when the Ch'ing Dynasty came to power, in 1644.

poem. When I chant them the spirit that gave them life emerges spontaneously from my paintings.

It is one and the same spiritual rhythm that imparts life to the poems and to the paintings. Both are manifestations of the underlying harmony. One of Shih T'ao's paintings is a translation of a dream of Su Tung-p'o's, which he describes in one of his poems. The dream was that he was chatting with his friend in a little mountain cottage during a heavy snowstorm. The vagueness of the scenery in the dream is recreated in the artist's work. Two men, lightly sketched, are sitting face to face by the window, drinking a glass of wine in celebration of their happy reunion after long years of separation. There is not much to be seen in the picture, just a few light strokes which serve, however, to bring out the reality of the poem.

Once spiritual reality is grasped, it can be expressed equally well by either poem or painting. This is what Su Tung-p'o meant when he said: "When I chant the poems of Mo-Chi (Wang Wei) I sense therein his paintings; when I gaze at his paintings I sense therein his poems. When we examine Wang Wei's work we find that Wang Wei himself realized that he was indeed a painter as well as a poet:

The present world [3] *took me for a poet.*
In my former life I must have been a master of painting.
I cannot cast off my old habits;
And it so happens that the people now know this too.

During our discussion of Chinese poetry we came to know Wang Wei as a man absorbed by the spirit of *Tao*.

[3] There are two versions of this line: *su shih*, former world, and *tang t'ai*, present world. My choice follows *Tang Shih's Chi shih*, or *Records of Poetry During the Tang Period*, by Chi Yu-kung.

His creative intuition penetrated through the outer shell of things to their inner reality. He had experienced nature's imageless, wordless, and soundless untouched primacy and therefore could make her invisible, integral beauty tangible to the senses either by means of rhymes and rhythm, or by form and color.

These artistic media are such that they would seem by their nature to impose conscious limitations. Yet when an artist has gained inner, deep freedom, he will transcend all measurements and rules and purely reflect nature's innate beauty. This idea is expressed in the following passage from the works of Chuang Tzu, which we have previously quoted in the chapter on creativity:

Those who rely upon the arc, the line, compasses and the square to make correct forms injure the natural construction of things. Those who use cords to bind and to glue to piece together interfere with the natural character of things. . . . There is an ultimate reality of things. Things in their ultimate reality are curved without the help of arcs, straight without lines, round without compasses, and rectangular without right angles. . . . In this manner all things create themselves from their own innermost reflections and none can tell how they came to do so (*Ch. 8*).

The idea of pure reflection as enunciated by the early Taoist philosopher became thereafter the guiding principle in painting and was adhered to throughout the centuries by all great artists. This is evidenced in the writings of Chang Yen-yuan, an art historian of the ninth century. Once Chang Yen-yuan was asked why the master Wu Tao-tsu (eighth century) could produce curves and arcs, and straight lines without using any kind of measuring devices. His answer was that

Wu Tao-tsu had become one with the universe and all things and that therefore his brush was no more his but had become the creative agent for all forms.

This fundamental principle of Chinese painting was further expounded by Shih T'ao in his *Hua Yü Lu,* or *Dialogue on Painting:*

Compasses and rulers can be used to make circles and squares. But in the universe there is a continual process by which circles and squares are created. If one can grasp the principle of the universe, one is freed from the necessity of using artifices, like compasses and rulers. Men are tied to artificial rules, which become obstructions and limitations. True method is born in the act of creation and is free from obstructions and limitations. When the artist comprehends the universe, the Tao painting will unfold *(Ch. 2).*

What then, is Tao-painting? We may, from what we have already said, define it as the spontaneous reflection from one's inner reality, unbound by arbitrary rules from without and undistorted by confusion and limitations from within. In this spontaneous reflection one's potentialities are set free and great creativity is achieved without artificial effort. This method of no-method in painting is the application of Taoist philosophy. As we know, *Tao* is the ontological experience by which subjective and objective reality are fused into one. This identification does not take place in the conscious realm through a logical process, but is that inner experience of which Chuang Tzu speaks when he says: "Heaven and Earth and I live together, and all things and I are one." This unity in multiplicity is invisible and unfathomable and its emergence is not intentional but natural and spontaneous.

The significance of unity rests upon the fact that infinite potentiality is manifest in particularity. When the painter, who is one with nature, seizes his brush to create the particular, his activity will be supported by all the vitality of universality. To illustrate this interrelationship we turn once again to the Buddhist's analogy of the lion, which we have cited previously in the chapter on Creativity. Each hair of the lion contains the potentialities of the whole lion, and therefore all the hairs of the lion have the potentialities of the infinitude of lions and this infinitude of lions is further contained within each single hair.

Thus, when creativity manifests itself, the potentialities of universality are far beyond the capacities of any individual. In the history of Chinese painting there are many instances given where artists claim that they lost themselves entirely in the act of painting. Wu Chen (fourteenth century), known as Mei-hua Tao-jen, or the Taoist of Plum Blossoms, once said, "When I begin to paint, I do not know that I am painting; I entirely forget that it is myself who holds the brush." He was indeed in that state of oneness of which Lao Tzu says, "Obtaining the One, all things live and grow." Thus, as in the case of Wu Chen, the finest work in Chinese painting was produced when all the potentialities of the universe went along with the painter's brush. Here we may recall the Channist's saying, "I lift my finger and the whole universe comes along with it."

As we have said before, creativity must also be understood in terms of another principle: the changeless within the ever-changing. Unity is both static and dynamic. In its static aspect it is the changeless; in its dynamic aspect it is the ever-changing. When the changeless remains within itself it is oneness, or nonbeing, the ground or reservoir of creativity. Changes are the manifestations of the changeless, which is boundless in space and endless in time, the primordial source of all potentialities in all things. It is from this abundant source that the Chinese artist draws his strength and by which his brush work is nourished. When Su Tung-p'o holds the brush he feels that potentialities issue forth like spring water from the ground, flowing with ease, covering a thousand miles a day. He admits that this quiet, murmuring stream cannot be defined. All he knows is that this inner stream "moves when it must move and ceases when it must cease." This inner stream, which moves and ceases, has its origin in the ground, the changeless within the ever-changing, the motionless within the constantly moving. The changeless within the changing, the unity within particularities are one and the same. Other names for them are nonbeing and reality. It is this nonbeing, or reality, that the Chinese painters are searching for through forms and colors and which they attempt to reveal through forms and colors. When the artist does succeed in revealing reality his inner being benefits as much by it as it would by meditation.

This concept of the ontological intuition of reality is shared by Taoist, Buddhist, and Confucianist. Tsung Ping (fifth century), an artist who was deeply influenced by both Confucianism and Taoism, applied this

idea of ontological intuition in painting and called it
Li, which to him meant reality, rather than principle
—the commoner meaning of the word. In Tsung Ping's
"Essay on the Painting of Landscapes" we read:

> *Li,* or Reality, is that which vision reacts to and mind
> meets. When artists translate this reality into painting and
> grasp its subtlety, others' eyes respond to this and others'
> minds meet in this. This reaction of one's vision and this
> penetration of one's mind are spirit in action. When this
> spiritual action is stirred Reality is attained. Even if one
> were to search for it in the depth of caves could one do
> more than this?

The importance of this revelation of reality in painting is repeatedly stressed by Chinese art critics. In
Chang Huai's *Treatise on Painting* we find a statement
to that effect:

> Only he who reaches Reality can follow Nature's spon-
> taneity and be aware of the subtlety of things, and his mind
> will be absorbed by them. His brush will secretly be in har-
> mony with movement and quiescence and all forms will
> issue forth. Appearances and substance are caught in one
> motion as the life breath reverberates through them. He
> who is ignorant of Reality becomes a slave of passion and
> his nature will be distorted by externalities. He sinks into
> confusion and is disturbed by thoughts of gain and loss.
> He is nothing more than a prisoner of brush and ink. How
> can he speak of genuine works of Heaven and Earth? [4]

Reality, or *Li,* from which all things develop, is referred to by Fu Tsai of the eighth century as *Ling Fu,*
or spiritual court, a term first used by Chuang Tzu. In
the psychological sense it means the depth of the unconscious. To reach this depth of the unconscious
means to reveal the potentialities of the spiritual court.

[4] Yü Chien-hua, *History of Chinese Painting,* Vol. 1, p. 233.

The paintings that reveal these potentialities are called *Tao*-paintings. When Fu Tsai saw Chang Tsao's paintings of pines and rocks, he expressed his admiration in the following words:

When I sense the vigor of Chang Tsao's painting, I see no longer a painting—I see *Tao*. When painting, he leaves behind mere skills and measurements and his thoughts vanish into the creative night. The things brought out are not from the consciousness of the eye and ear, but from the Spiritual Court. What he achieves in his heart is made known by his hand.[5]

When the artist enters the invisible realm of creativity he uncovers the potentialities that are hidden in the spiritual court. To reach the state of no-thought, according to the Taoist, means to reach the realm of creativity. When the Chinese artist says that he enters the spiritual court he speaks of the ontological experience, the state of no-thought. This experience leads inevitably to the interfusion of subjective and objective reality. This interfusion initiates the process of creativity, which in turn establishes unity in multiplicity, the changeless in the ever-changing. The artist who has reached this state of oneness is supported by all the powers inherent in multiplicities and changes, and his work will be far beyond what his ego-form self could accomplish. Such a reflection of strength from the center of his being, however powerful it is, is completely nonintentional and effortless. Robert Henri (1865-1929), speaking of modern art, expresses somewhat the same idea:

The object, which is back of every true work of art, is the attainment of a state of being, a state of high function-

5 *Ibid.,* p. 139.

ing, a more than ordinary moment of existence. In such moments activity is inevitable, and whether this activity is with brush, pen, chisel, or tongue, its result is but a by-product of this state, a trace, the footprint of the state.[6]

The work of art is, indeed, the by-product of a state of high functioning. This state of spiritual exaltation is fundamental to creative activity, while skills and measurements are secondary. It is the manifestation of an ontological experience. The great painter Ku K'ai-chih[7] (c. 344-406) points out that the purpose of painting is *chu'an shen,* or the revelation of the spirit. He says:

Forms are used to reveal the spirit; when it is lost, one deviates from the principle of discarding the "fishing net and the snare[8] and the purpose of painting is missing. . . . Even though there be light and shade in the painting, nothing is better than to communicate with its spirit when one gazes at it.

Wang Wei[9] (fifth century critic) stresses the same idea: "When the spirit is not revealed in the form, what is carried by the form is not in action." What is in motion is revealed through form, but is itself not the form. When spirit is not in motion, it is the unrevealed

[6] Pantheon Books: *Artists on Art,* p. 401.
[7] Ku K'ai-chih (344-406) left two essays, one discussing the method of painting, the other a description of the famous landscape with the Taoist Heavenly Teacher. The quotation is from the first essay. His paintings are among the earliest preserved.
[8] A reference to Chuang Tzu's saying: "The fishing net serves to catch fish. Let us take the fish and forget the net. The snare serves to catch the rabbit. Let us take the rabbit and forget the snare."
[9] Wang Wei is the author of *Hsü Hüa,* or *Discussions on Painting,* one of the earliest writings of its sort. He himself was a painter. In the English transliteration of the spelling his name is the same as that of the famous poet-painter of the eighth century, but the Chinese character for his first name, Wei, is different and carries the meaning "invisible." The poet-painter's name Wei is a transliteration of the first syllable of the Sanskrit word *Vimalakirti.*

reality in the form; when in motion, it vibrates in the vision of the beholder. Early critics refer to both aspects of art, the visible and the invisible, with the word *shên*. When this word *shên* was used to describe the function of motion in painting, it apparently fell short of carrying the idea of unceasing motion. Therefore critics began to use a more complete term, *shên yün,* or spiritual rhythm, when they spoke of *shên* in motion. *Shên yün* was used for the first time in the biography of Wang Chin-hung, which is contained in the *History of the (Liu) Sung Dynasty.*

In the year 478 the Emperor Shun, of Liu Sung, praised Wang Chin-hung, a great scholar and statesman, for his elegant and plain spiritual rhythm, or *shên yün.* He said that "although he was highly honored as a court official, his mind contemplated that which is beyond the mundane world. His lucid light and genuine manner inspired the people and purified their spirit." This lucid light and genuine manner were manifestations of his inner power shining forth from the center of his being. Their beauty moved the emperor and inspired the people. In a work of art or poetry *shên yün* is that which is in the form and also that which goes beyond it to the beholder. Ssu-k'ung Tu (ninth century), a critic of poetry, says in his *Collection of Essays* (second chapter) that a plum is that which ends in sourness, and a grain of salt is that which ends in saltiness. We could do without sourness and saltiness in our food—however, the delight of the taste is beyond sourness and saltiness. A later critic commented on the question, "What is beyond sourness and saltiness?" "It is the taste beyond the taste; the taste beyond the taste is Spiritual Rhythm."

In his writings on painting Su Tung-p'o shares this idea of beyondness, when he says: "He who bases his evaluation of a painting on the likeness of forms makes his judgment immature as that of a child. Likewise, he who, when writing a poem, insists on its form, is surely far from being a poet." The true artist, as well as the true poet, is not concerned with the likeness of form, but aims at bringing forth the rhythm that pulsates within it, and then is carried beyond to the beholder.

Chang Seng-yu of the sixth century, famous for his dragon paintings, may serve as an example. He is said to have left the eyes of the dragon untouched up to the last moment. The reason for this odd procedure was given by a later commentator who claimed that as soon as the eyes were painted the dragons would fly away! Thus the eyes were kept to the very last. This fanciful explanation illustrates the fact that Chang Seng-yu's dragons were exceedingly lifelike. As he painted, he was in contact with the powerful cosmic forces at play in the universe. As he was, other artists too were becoming increasingly aware of the all-pervading cosmic rhythm and they began using the more appropriate term *ch'i yün*, or breath rhythm, instead of *shên yün*, or spiritual rhythm. It is interesting that the first and most fundamental principle of the six canons set forth by Hsieh Ho of the late fifth century is *ch'i yün sheng tung*, which may be translated "breath rhythm is lifelike." The further the art of painting developed the more frequently *ch'i yün* was used in preference to *shên yün*.

The word *ch'i* appears for the first time in the earliest Taoist classic, where Lao Tzu says, "Ten thousand things carry *yin* and embrace *yang;* through unification by *ch'i* they achieve harmony" (Ch. 42). Hsiung Shih-li explains: "That which is *yin* indicates form; that which is *yang* indicates spirit. Ten thousand things, all carrying a form and hiding a spirit, are in motion with the multitude. When *yin* and *yang* harmonize the ten thousand things are transformed. This is called the union of *ch'i.*" [10] Thus we see that it is the function of *ch'i* to unify the appearance (*yin*) with the reality (*yang*) of ten thousand things. In painting *ch'i* is that which reveals the objective reality of the form. In other words, *ch'i* makes the painting exist for itself and moves it beyond itself. It is what Jacques Maritain calls "immanent action" in his exposition of creative intuition. "The action of the poem," he explains, "is what the poem does—an elan or notion which develops it, and through which within itself it asserts itself beyond itself." [11] Hsiung Shih-li stresses the intrinsic function of *ch'i.* But it also has an extrinsic function, which is called "transitive action" by Maritain—"through which one thing modifies another." In the second chapter of the *Tao Te Ching Lao Tzu* speaks of the modification of opposites which is to bring out the reverberation of the life breath.

A number of basic guide lines have been laid down by Chinese artists for the composition of a painting, such as *hsü shih,* or vacant space versus solid; *ming an,* or darkness versus light; *kan shih,* or dryness versus

---

[10] Hsiung Shih-li, *Yuan Ju,* or *Origin of Confucianism,* Sec. II, p. 36, 1956.
[11] Maritain, *op. cit.,* p. 255.

wetness, and many others. In Hsun Tsu-yung's *Kuei Shih Chin Liang,* or *Ferry Boat of Painting,* the author, commenting on *hsü shih,* says:

> In the composition of a picture there must be spiritual breath coming and leaving without hindrance. Generally speaking, when the left side is vacant, the right side should be solid; when the right side is vacant, then the left side should be solid.

In his book, *Hua Ch'uan,* or *The Net of Painting,* Ta Chung-k'uang relates "solidity" and "vacancy" with the ideas of light and darkness:

> White vacancy is *yang,* or light; solid ink wash is *yin,* or darkness. When there are no wrinkles on the top of the mountain, this signifies light. When there is a heavy ink wash in the valley, this signifies the darkness of the shadow. . . . If there are not sufficient wrinkles, a heavy wash is used to reveal the essence of the rock. If there are enough wrinkles, a light wash is used to produce the life rhythm.

K'ung Yen-shih in his *Hua Chü,* or *The Secret of Painting,* further explains the subtlety of applying the principles of solidity and vacancy:

> . . . to draw trees or rocks the solid stroke is used; to draw clouds and mists the vacant stroke is used. Through that which is vacant the solid is moved and that which is solid becomes vacant. Thus the entire picture will be full of the life rhythm.

Although the proper distribution of vacant and solid areas and the other aforementioned techniques have to be observed by the artist in the composition of a painting, there are other means at his disposal. *Pi* and *mo,* or brush stroke and ink wash, are generally considered as the two fundamentals in bringing out the breath rhythm. In one of his six canons, Hsieh Ho explains *pi fa*, or the method of the brush stroke. He says that the brush stroke should have bone structure. Such a stroke, he maintains, is something more than just a line, since it blends dynamic strength with spiritual reverberation. Ching Hao of the tenth century lists the brush stroke and the ink wash as two of the six essentials. He declares the *ch'i* is produced "when the artist's mind does not interfere with the free movement of the brush and thus spontaneously produces the picture without fear." Then he defines the brush stroke: "Although the brush stroke follows certain rules—moves, turns, changes and penetrates—it must not be limited by its quality or form but be as if it were flying and flowing." The spontaneous movement of the brush, which reveals the breath rhythm, is not merely a technical achievement, but the immediate reflection from the painter's inmost being. Things have their reality and will participate in the subjectivity of the painter when he allows them to captivate him. The great artist's brush stroke is nothing less than the subjective agent for the expression of objective reality.

Kuo Jo-hsü, in his *Tu Hua Chien Wen Chih,* or *Experience of Painting,* points out:

In painting *ch'i yün,* or breath rhythm, originates in the roaming mind and the spiritual color is produced by the brush stroke. As long as the mind remains in the deep undisturbed reservoir, it sleeps and is unseen; but when it awakens, its activity is vigilance and vital tension. For their transmission to the beholder vigilance and vital tension depend upon the breath rhythm.

Describing Ku K'ai-chih's brush work, Chang Yen-yuan says: "The brush work of Ku K'ai-chih is full of strength and vigor, moving unceasingly. His strokes are revolving and far-reaching, their tune is free and at ease. They move like the blustering gale and the swift lightning." Commenting on the brush work of Wu Tao-tzu and Chang Seng-yu, he continues thus:

Their brush works are the media of the divine, produced by God. The illuminating spirit is infinite. Others are striving for refinement of perception, but Wu and Chang condense the brush stroke into a few essential dots and lines. Others are strictly limited by the likeness of forms, but Wu and Chang are free from this common vulgar taste. When they draw the bending curve or straight sword, the vertical pillar or horizontal beam, they do not depend on measurements and rulers. Curly whiskers or cloudy hair are made several feet long, flying and moving. The root of each hair in the flesh can be seen. The strokes are full of strength.[12]

When the subtlety of the brush work reveals strength and vigor, the breath rhythm will be fully expressed. To better convey the subtlety of the rhythm various styles of strokes were developed. For example, when Liang K'ai tried to reveal the inner unlimited dynamism and great sensitivity of the poet Li Po, he used the so-called simplified stroke of *chien pi,* and he succeeded well in expressing the great poet's personality: A slanting stroke for the eyelid; a dark dot for the brilliancy of the eyeball; a fine line for the pointed nose to convey the feeling of straightforwardness; a few waving strings for the whiskers to bring out the dignity of the venerable old gentleman; and some net-like lines for the hair knot, typical of the ancient scholar. All these simple strokes, added together, give

[12] Chang Yen-yuan, *Li-t'ai Ming-hua Chi,* or *Records of the Famous Paintings in Former Dynasties.*

us a lifelike picture of the genius of Li Po. The "simplified stroke" was widely used by *Chan* Buddhist and
Taoist artists. Wu Wei (1459-1508), who often used
his Taoist name, Lesser Fairy, painted a branch of
plum blossoms with only a mere handful of strokes, yet
the characteristics of the plum branch vibrate forth
strongly from the lines (Plate 1).

As long as the artists painted on silk they used the
wet stroke, or *shih-pi,* but later, when the rice paper
came into use, they applied the dry stroke, or *k'o-pi,* to
take advantage of the rough surface of the paper. The
inventor of this style was Huang Kung-wang. In his
famous painting, *Chih-lan Chü,* or Mansion of the Orchids (Plate 2), the artist used the dry brush for rocks,
trees, and mountains. Osvald Siren gives the following
evaluation of this painting:

The beauty and significance of this picture is entirely a
matter of the brush work, difficult to describe, but evident
to a close observer. The design is finely built, yet the forms
are not strictly outlined but rather dissolved in a play of
light and shades suggested by a rich scale of tonal values.
The ground tone of grassy hills is a light grey indicated by
thin washes and subtle touches of a tenuous brush. It is
not uniform, but modulated, so as to follow the shapes,
and over this is spread a rich scale of darker tones varying
from deep grey to jet black and mostly applied with short
horizontal and vertical strokes. They represent the trees
and the shrubs as growing in the folds of the ground and
have a distinct structural quality which contributes to the
tectonic effect of the whole thing. The interplay of tones
is thus accentuated by the brush strokes in a way which
leads our thoughts to certain drawings by Van Gogh,
though the Chinese painting has more unified atmosphere.
The comparison may serve to emphasize its surprisingly
modern character, though it does not touch the essentials
in Huang Kung-wang's little picture, which ranks in truth

among the noblest of all Chinese ink paintings that have been preserved. Seeing it we can understand to some extent why Huang Kung-wang was for generations hailed as the foremost among the masters of monochrome landscape-painting. This little picture reveals the driving force of a master spirit in every stroke and makes such a pronouncement comprehensible.[13]

The dry-stroke style, introduced by Huang Kung-wang, was adopted by other great masters, such as Wang Meng, Wu Chen, and Ni Tsan,[14] and these were followed by later artists. In contrast to mediocre paintings, which leave the beholder with a taste of the vulgar, these dry-stroke paintings of the great masters impress the beholder with their simplicity and purity.

The discussion of the brush stroke leads us inevitably to the discussion of Chinese calligraphy. It is obvious that technically calligraphy and painting are similarly conditioned: both use brush and ink, silk and paper; both follow certain rules for moving the brush. An often striking resemblance between the symbols of the calligraphist and the forms of the painter points to the same origin. But in addition to this outer relationship there exists a close inner relationship between these two arts, which is the result of their common philosophical background. The following statement from Chang Huai Kuan's *Shu Tuan,* or *Evaluation of Calligraphy,* confirms this assertion:

Those who really understand calligraphy look only into the spiritual rhythm but not at the forms of the script.

[13] Osvald Siren, *Chinese Painting: Great Masters and Principles,* Vol. IV, p. 67.
[14] Huang Kung-wang (1268-1354), Wang Meng (ca. 1309-1385), Wu Chen (1280-1354) and Ni Tsan (1301-1374) are considered the four great masters in the Yuan Period according to Yu Chien-hua's *History of Chinese Painting.*

When we purify our minds and look into the Source, nothing escapes our insight. . . . If the brush work does not
come from one's inner reality it lacks spiritual rhythm.

A later section of his book, in which he explains the
grass script, reads like a discussion of the philosophy of
painting. He says:

There is a difference between K'ai Shu and Tsao Shu,
"formal script" and "grass script." Whenever the calligraphist expresses an idea in the formal script such idea
comes to an end with the completion of his writing, but
when he completes his writing in the grass script, the
movement seems to go on. Sometimes this script seems
like the condensation and dispersion of mists and clouds,
and sometimes it seems like the stroke of lightning or
the floating stream of stars. It has the spiritual bones for
its substance; it is in a permanent state of transformation. . . . No matter how noble the critics be, they cannot esteem it highly enough; no matter how well trained
in mathematics, they cannot measure its strength. When
we apply the action of non-action our brush work will be
comparable to the works of Nature; when we identify our
writing with the true nature of things we follow the fundamental principle of creativity. No one knows how this is
done. It must be comprehended by our heart; it cannot
be expressed in words.

I shall discuss the philosophy of calligraphy more
fully at the end of this chapter since there is much
more to be said about it. Summing up our discussion of
the brush stroke, I want to point out that even in calligraphy the stress is not on the likeness of form but on
its inner reality—its spiritual rhythm.

We have learned that the two basic techniques in
Chinese painting are *pi* and *mo,* or brush stroke and
ink-wash. Along with the development of the brush
stroke and ink-wash came a more powerful expression

of the breath rhythm. As, in early days, color was used almost exclusively, the literary term for painting was *tan t'sing*, meaning red and green. Although there were a few great painters who succeeded in revealing spiritual reality through this medium, the average artist would use color merely as a means of presenting things in their outer appearance. Wang Wei, the great poet-painter of the eighth century whom we have mentioned earlier, began using the monochrome ink-wash instead of sharp cutting lines, as he found it to be a more suitable medium for the expression of spiritual reality. His object in painting mountains and trees was to reveal what is within them rather than to give a detailed description of their outer appearance.

Wang Wei's ink-wash is called *p'o mo*, meaning penetrating or breaking ink, because by breaking the confining outer form reality is laid bare. This monochrome ink painting is decidedly an advance over the color painting, which is intent on imitating appearances. Let us listen to what Sheng Tsung-ch'ien has to say on the subject of monochrome ink-painting:

The color of a painting is not red, white, green or purple as ordinarily conceived. It is the shade seen between lightness and darkness. He who grasps this idea will reveal through his brush the Nature of things; the distance will be demarcated, the spirit will be set forth, and the scenery and the objects will be clear and beautiful. The reverberation of the life breath actually depends upon the proper manner of applying the ink-wash, which gives the picture great luminosity.[15]

Since in traditional painting the artist was limited by the use of colors and held to restricting rules and

15 Shen Tsung-ch'ien, active between 1770-1817, the author of *Chieh Chou Hsueh Hua,* or *The Study of the Painting of Chieh Chou.*

measurements, he could never fully reveal spiritual reality. Therefore Wang Wei's *p'o mo* was an important step toward the liberation of spirituality in painting. An even more radical step in that direction was the introduction of the splashing ink, or *p'oh mo* which was developed by Wang Hsia, of the eighth century. His paintings are the immediate reflection from within by means of the splashing ink with only a few straightforward strokes added. In the execution of this style the painter's brush moves swiftly, absolutely free from restricting rules. There is no hesitation or deliberation when he handles the brush. Hand and mind are unified, there being no interference from the intellect or the emotions. It was said that Wang Hsia's brush sometimes waves and sometimes sweeps. The color of his ink is sometimes light and sometimes dark. Following the splotches of the ink he shapes them into mountains, rocks, clouds, and water. His action is so swift as if it were from Heaven. Spontaneously his hand responds and his mind follows. All at once clouds and mists are completed; wind and rain are painted. Yet, when one looks carefully, one cannot find any marks of demarcation in the ink.[16]

Wang Hsia's spontaneous and unrestrained monochrome ink-painting marks a new era in the history of Chinese painting. His style was enthusiastically adopted by Liang Kai, Mu Ch'i, Mi Fei, and many other artists. This type of painting can be well understood from a statement made by Chang Tsao, a painter who lived a little earlier than Wang Hsia, during the *Tang* period. He painted with a stumpy brush and used the palm of his hand to spread the ink on the silk.

16 Yü Chien-hua, *op. cit.,* p. 112.

When asked about the method or rules that he followed, his answer was: "Outwardly, I follow the Creativity of Nature; inwardly I gain from the Source of my heart." To follow the law of nature is to be free from human limitations and confining rules. To obtain something from the source of one's heart is the process of self-realization. What he reveals in his paintings comes from the primordial source. His work is the manifestation of an ontological experience, which emerges from the depth of the unconscious. Therefore Fu Tsai, as I mentioned before, said that Chang Tsao's paintings were revelations of Tao.

P'oh mo, developed by the Tang artists, was widely adopted by later painters. When we look at Yin Yü-chien's landscapes we can detect at a glance that he has broken with tradition. There are hardly any brush strokes used except to indicate a human figure or the corner of a temple roof. The rest of the picture— mountains, trees, clouds and rivers—are done with broad splashing ink. Although the straightforwardness of the brush work indicates the immediate reflection from the painter's inmost being, it is through the various shades of splashing ink that the moving breath is brought out. This idea of bringing out the moving breath through shades of splashing ink was taken up by Mi Fei (1051-1107) and his followers with some modifications. When we look at his landscapes (Plate 3, for example) we have the feeling that the breath moves unceasingly from light to gray, from gray to dark, and again from dark back to gray and light. As to composition, Mi Fei did not entirely break away from tradition, but his ink-wash reveals the reverberation of the breath.

The reverberation of breath is merely a manifestation; its aim is to reveal the reality of things. In using the technique of the ink-wash and the splashing-ink the artist may indulge in mere shading of ink and fail to fulfill his greater purpose. And painters who used the simplified and dry-stroke techniques often missed the spiritual reality of their creations by concentrating merely on the strength and refinement of their techniques. Wu Wei, a later great master of the simplified stroke style, who used swift, tyrannical strokes, often fails to reveal the depth of the nature of things. Although the reverberation of the breath may convey to us impressions of strength, beauty, and elegance, these are merely manifestations of reality, but not reality itself. The highest achievement of the artist lies a step further, i.e., not in the mere revelation of strength or beauty or elegance. It is the painting of creative innocence. These paintings do not make any claim to beauty, power, elegance. Instead they are totally simple, childlike in their innocence. This absolute simplicity makes us realize that the artist's mind was in the state of nonbeing when he painted the picture. The famous painting entitled "Six Persimmons," attributed to Mu Ch'i (thirteenth century) is a pure reflection of nonbeing (Plate 4). It expresses the innocence of *P'o*, the uncarved block mentioned in the chapter on Sympathy.

When we gaze at the picture of these six persimmons we are not impressed with the motif—the contours of ordinary fruit—nor is there any unusual beauty or strength traceable to technical skill. Rather, these six simple shapes make us visualize the artist's state of mind at the moment he took up his brush. It is obvious that he was not concerned about presenting a motif that would have a strong appeal for Chinese traditional sentiment, such as plum blossoms flowering in the snow, or the lotus flowers waving gracefully in a light breeze on the surface of a lake, or the steadfast evergreen pine that symbolizes the strong and upright character of the gentleman. All such motifs have definite characteristics while the six common persimmons have none to speak of. These shapes are merely an expression of the artist's innocence; they are the by-product of his inner experience. This uncarved block painting is a good illustration of what the Chinese critics call *san-mei,* or *samadhi,* painting. Such a painting, which emerges from the state of nonbeing, the state of non-differentiation, or no-knowledge, is a painting of the first principle. It is this philosophy of the first principle which Shih Tao recommended to his nephew in his inscription on his model painting (Plate 5). He says, "One who judges painting should proceed as if he were discussing Zen. He must not hold on to differentiating knowledge, but enter into the philosophy of the first principle. Then he will become a great master of the art. . . ."

The model landscape that Shih Tao painted for his nephew contains three leafless trees, some common dwarf bamboo groves, with a little rocky hill for background. Nothing in the picture can be said to be either powerful or beautiful. There is no vivid breath movement as in the mountain and mist paintings of Mi Fei, nor are there any reverberations from dry strokes as in Huang Kung-wang's painting of the Mansion of the Orchids. All that we get from this picture is the native primacy of trees, dwarf bamboo groves, meaningless hills, rocky banks. To this uncarved block quality nothing else is added by the artist. This kind of painting is done when the artist's mind is in the state of no-knowledge, or nonbeing.

However, this state of nonbeing does not only manifest itself as native primacy but also as the Heavenly light. When in meditation, the state of emptiness is achieved and the Heavenly light emerges. As Chuang Tzu said, "It is in the empty chamber that the light is produced." The emptiness from which the Heavenly light is produced is not emptiness in the relative sense. It is the absolute void, which is neither empty nor non-empty. When one reaches this stage, one's inner being is in the state of ontological transparency, which we speak of as the Heavenly light. When the artist achieves such ontological transparency and manifests it in his brush work, his painting will reveal purity and emptiness. In his *Treatise on Painting* Wang Yü interprets *sanmei* as *ts'ing k'ung,* or purity and emptiness.[17]

It is known that Ni Tsan's[18] paintings have been highly esteemed by both critics and painters. Yet the sublime quality of his work was beyond the verbal capacity of the critics, and his imitators had to confess that they were not able to reach Ni Tsan's height. Although Ni Tsan was a master of brush and ink, his skills alone did not win him the high praise of critics and painters alike. There was something in his paintings that none could describe or imitate since the secret of his achievement was hidden in his heart. From that illumined chamber he reflected the Heavenly light to his paintings and it was this transparency that enthralled the

17 *Tung Chuang Lun Hua,* or *Treatise on Painting,* by Wang Yü (active c. 1680-1729).
18 Ni Tsan (1301-1374), one of the three great masters of painting based upon Taoist philosophy, as mentioned in footnote 1.

beholder. He painted simply to express his inner serenity; therefore whatever he painted—be it trees, branches of the bamboo, rocky banks—all became reflections of his inner exalted state.

Once Ni Tsan explained why he painted bamboo:

I-chung (the name of a friend) always likes my bamboo paintings. I am painting bamboo to release my inner serenity. How can I care for likeness and unlikeness; for abundant or scattered leaves; for slanting or straight branches? Perhaps after having worked for a long time people may even take them for hemp or reeds. Why should I try to convince them that they are bamboo? [19]

When Ni Tsan speaks of releasing his inner serenity he means that he mirrors ontological purity and clarity through his brush work (Plate 6). When the bamboo is painted to resemble the actual bamboo the artist is attached to objective actuality (Plate 7). When the bamboo is painted to represent the artist's own character as a gentleman he is attached to subjective ideality (Plate 8). Ni Tsan's bamboo painting transcends objective and subjective attachment. He is free from the imitation of objective actuality and also free from subjective projection. Being nonattached to either realistic objectivity or idealistic subjectivity, his work is the product of absolute emptiness, or *k'ung*. By releasing his inner transparency, his painting is permeated with ontological purity—*ts'ing*. *Ts'ing* and *k'ung* are attributes of *sanmei,* and therefore we can say that in Ni Tsan's painting there is *sanmei*. To support our evaluation of Ni Tsan, we may quote Shih t'ao's comments given in the colophon of the painting that he copied from Ni Tsan:

[19] Yü Chien-hua, op. cit. Vol. II, p. 32.

The great master Ni's painting is just like the sand in waves and pebbles in the stream, which roll and tumble spontaneously and naturally follow the water. However, there is emptiness and purity which penetrate into the beholder, just as the cool breeze. . . .

Ni Tsan's biographer praised him, saying that in the center of his being the transparent ice, the crystal snow, and the floating mists and clouds were incoming and outgoing. This is what makes his brush work reach the utmost. From his biography we learn that one day he divided his property among his friends and relatives. He himself stayed in a junk and sailed on the rivers and lakes. He spent his time visiting friends, making poems, and painting pictures. This simple and carefree life is the reflection of his innermost being. The following poem and its introduction give us an idea of his Taoist training:

Master Hsun-chung built a hall for meditation at the eastern gate of Wu Hsieh and called it "The Temple of Hsun Wên." It is a quiet place, spacious and light, where I rest. . . . I discard all mundane affairs and let my mind roam in a world of simplicity and purity. Early in the morning, after refreshing myself, I concentrate on the sutras. All day long I keep company with the ancient Taoists. I forget myself and reach *Tao.* How joyful I am when I have obtained *Tao.* At the foot of the Hsi Shen Hill is a spring, sweet and clear, different from ordinary water. The hill is only a few miles west of the temple. In the morning and in the evening I carry the spring water home and make tea. After I have studied Taoist books I drink this water. I am full of joy and thus I sing:

How profoundly silent is the temple of Tao!
Boundless and infinite, it is the dwelling place of the divine.
The light-hall is wide and high, yet awed by silence.

Trees with colored leaves are flourishing and spreading.
Forgetful of words I roam and rest here.
I have discarded the world of fame and profit.
How elegant is the morning sun shining on the rafters and eaves.
How cool are the terrace and pond after the rain.
I burn incense to break the deep silence,
And drink the spring water and relax in joy.
I penetrate into the wonders of Tao,
And chant the ancient sutras.
When my mind is at ease my spirit is gay.
When understanding is gained, there is nothing left to comprehend.
Who can say that the realm of Tao *is far from us?*
How tranquil it is—as at the beginning of Heaven and Earth.[20]

This poem shows Ni Tsan's devotion to the study of *Tao* and his attainment in meditation. He had reached the state of tranquillity. As he himself says: "Who says that the realm of *Tao* is far away? How tranquil it is— as at the beginning of Heaven and Earth." The origin of Heaven and Earth is the state of nondifferentiation, which Lao Tzu describes as "silent, invisible, unchanging, standing as One, unceasing, ever revolving—able to be Mother of the world."

Through the study of *Tao* Ni Tsan had achieved the ontological experience, the goal of the student of *Tao*. From his declaration that painting was to him simply an avenue for expressing inner serenity, it is not hard for us to understand that his way of living was beyond the limits of ordinary men's lives. His brush work was one of the by-products of his self-cultivation. It was the manifestation of ontological experience. In his brush work he identifies ontological experience with creative

[20] Ni Tsan, *Ni Yün-lin Shih Chi,* or *Collection of Poems of Ni Tsan* (Yün-lin is the pen name of Ni Tsan), Vol. I.

intuition. His innermost self is pure and empty, and his brush work reflects this pureness and emptiness. To him a tree, a branch of bamboo, and a rocky bank are not conceptual assertions or actual imitations but the transparency of things through which he expressed his own transparency. His inner serenity is revealed by revealing the serenity of things. However, the awakening of objective serenity cannot take place without the awakening of subjective serenity first. What is this awakening of subjective serenity? It is the achievement of *Tao*.

The manifestation of *Tao* in brush work is twofold, as mentioned before. Ni Tsan's bamboo paintings convey Heavenly radiance, while Mu Ch'i's persimmons illustrate creative innocence: the uncarved block. Both aspects are highly esteemed by Chinese artists. Some painters reveal more of the transparency of radiance; others reveal more of the simplicity of innocence. Two great masters of the seventeenth century, Shih t'ao and Pa-ta Shan-jen,[21] may serve as good illustrations. The former's work is permeated with light (Plate 9); the latter's work has absorbed the essence of innocence (Plate 10). These two qualities are carried over even to the present-day painting. If we analyze Ch'i Pai-shih's[22] brush work we find both qualities, transparency and innocence (Plates 11 and 12). Thus we see that the emphasis placed either on transparency or innocence depends on the artist's prevailing mood.

In the moment of creation, when the artist is in the unconscious of conscious, he reflects the innocence of

21 Pa-ta Shan-jen is Chu Ta's pen name. He was born around 1626 and lived more than seventy-five years. He was a descendant of Ming nobility and after the rise of the Manchus he became a monk.
22 Ch'i Pai-shih, 1861-1957.

the uncarved block; when he is in the conscious of the unconscious he reflects the transparency of Heavenly radiance. Both aspects represent the state of no-thought, or nonbeing. (When the artist achieves the state of no-thought he reflects either the unconscious of consciousness or the conscious of unconsciousness.) No matter whether the reflection is innocence or transparency, it is free from the conditions of subjectivity and objectivity. Yet it reveals them both.

If the artist is free merely from subjectivity he is still trapped in the imitation of actuality. If he is free merely from objectivity he remains a slave of ideality. The highest achievement of Chinese painting is not conditioned either by subjectivity or by objectivity. It is rather through the objectivity of the brush work that the subjectivity of the artist is revealed. And it is through the subjective tranquillity of the artist that the objective tranquillity of the brush work is uncovered. Within subjectivity there is objectivity; within objectivity there is subjectivity. In the Taoist phrase, the universe and I are one. This oneness is the expression of philosophical speculation, but in terms of modern art it would be the unity of consonance. George Rowley observes: "In China, as early as the Sung period, the principle of consonance was given a profound meaning by being linked up with the philosophical speculation as to the oneness of the *Tao* which permeated the universe."[23] It is true, indeed, that ever since the tenth century life and culture of the Chinese people were deeply influenced by both Taoist and Buddhist philosophy. This profound meaning, given and enjoyed by the great minds, was transmitted to the works of great

[23] George Rowley: *Principles of Chinese Painting*, p. 53.

artists. Thus Chinese painting is not merely a product of technical skill but it is basically an achievement of a high level of self-cultivation, without which creative intuition cannot emerge. When we discussed Chinese poetry we identified creative intuition with ontological experience. This also holds true for Chinese painting. When creative intuition and ontological experience become one, great works of art are produced.

As we have mentioned previously, Chinese calligraphy and painting rest on the same philosophical foundation. Before we come to the conclusion of this chapter on painting, I would like to say a little about Chinese calligraphy.

The animation of the brush stroke aimed at by the Chinese painter was primarily considered an essential element in Chinese calligraphy. According to the teachings of the Chinese calligraphists, the brush in its movement may strike swiftly as a sword, or proceed steadily as a garden toad; it may draw out a fine line as if pulling out a silk thread from a cocoon, or make a dot as if laying down a heavy rock; it may wind a curve as if stretching out an ancient steel bow. All these activities of the brush convey that which is beyond a line or a group of lines. The inexpressible subtlety of the artist's brush brings out the wonders of the spiritual rhythm. Many of the great masters of painting, such as Chang Chih-ho, Mi Fei, Chao Meng-fu,[24] and many others were also outstanding calligraphists. The great master of the stroke style in Chinese painting, Wu Tao-tzu, received his training from Chang Hsü, the

[24] Chao Meng-fu, also known as Chao Chih-ang, the great calligraphist of the thirteenth century and originator of the so-called Chao Style, is famous for his horse paintings.

great calligraphist of the grass style. His paintings owed their vital strength to the dynamic movements of his brush. The subtlety and power that his brush expressed were, no doubt, the harvest of calligraphy. This indicates that the training of calligraphy is always carried over to painting.

However, the relationship between Chinese calligraphy and painting is not limited to the similarity of external forms, such as the method for beginners of painting bamboo. The first lesson in bamboo painting points out that three styles of calligraphy can be used in the brush work of painting bamboo; for the stem one should use the style of *Li Shu,* or official style;[25] for the twigs one should use the style of *T'sao Shu,* or grass style;[26] and for the leaves the style of *K'ai Shu,* or formal style.[27] The application of these various styles of calligraphy to painting stresses the similarity of the outer shapes of the stroke. When one studies the subject a little further one finds out that these identifications of forms are superficial and limited. Such striking similarity in outer forms does not reveal the inner relationship that exists between the two Chinese arts. It is only from a more intimate study that we can see just what this is.

When we examine ancient Chinese scripts we find that many ideographic symbols reveal the author's poetic intuition, which later on was to play an impor-

[25] *Li Shu* was first developed during the third century b.c. by Ch'eng Miao. A stroke contains varied shapes, which appear as square and straight instead of rounded or curved.
[26] *T'sao Shu* was developed for rough draft writing. The stroke is grassy, signifying free-flowing and uncurbed movement.
[27] *K'ai Shu* was developed after *Li Shu,* by the end of the Han Period. The stroke contains some elegantly slender shapes and alternatively broad and heavy ones.

tant role in Chinese art. For instance, the symbol for *ming,* or light, was not developed solely from outer observation of the Moon outside a window, but the motif that is chosen points as well to an inner experience. To express the idea of light a number of other symbols might have been chosen—the rising sun, or fire, for example—but evidently none corresponded exactly to the originator's prevailing mood. These ideas betray his poetic feeling, when the inventor of these ancient symbols held the instrument for making the marks on a fragment of bone or shell. Because the drawing of the Moon outside the window conveys the creative intuition of its inventor—when perhaps he sat by the window and gazed at the Moon shining in the dark night.

We might take another illustration to support our contention that creative intuition was at work in the ancient inventors of Chinese script. The character *hsien,* meaning leisure, quiescence, or being at ease, is composed of two parts: a closed door and the Moon. Such a drawing indicates the inventor's feeling when he gazed at the moonlight streaming through closed doors. The creative impulse in such a case is scarcely differentiable between the calligraphist and the painter. The awakening of the creative intuition can be applied to both arts. Even much later, when calligraphy had developed into various refinements of style, the basic principle of calligraphy set forth by the great master can still be applied to painting as well. Li Ssu (third century), inventor of the Small Seal Style,[28] gives us the following on the philosophy of calligraphy:

[28] The Seal Style can be classified into two categories: the Great Seal Style and the Small Seal Style. Traditionally we believe that the Great Seal was standardized during the eighth century B.C. and the Small Seal was created by Li Ssu during the third century B.C.

The work of calligraphy is fine and subtle. Through *Tao* it achieves harmony with nature. . . . One must leave one's stroke to spontaneity and cannot make it over again. When you move the brush gradually toward the end of the stroke you will feel like a fish who enjoys swimming in the running stream. When you swing the strokes outward it is as if the clouds were rising from behind the mountain. Sometimes the line is curled; sometimes straight; sometimes light; sometimes heavy. All these lines rely upon one's imagination, which leads to the Truth.[29]

Here we have the idea of *Tao* first mentioned as the basic principle of calligraphy, the harmony of the executor of the brush and nature. However, Li Ssu's statement is a fragmentary one as it has come down to us; sketchy as it is, though, it is an important one. Later, in the second century, we have Ts'ai Yung, a great calligraphist and scholar, who laid down principles of the art of writing based upon the idea of one's inner serenity as a source of creative impulse. The motif of the writing, he said, emerges from within. As he states in his "Essay on Brush-Work," calligraphy is a releasing of one's self. When one takes up the brush he should set himself free to be natural and spontaneous. This is achieved through meditation and contemplation. From quiescence one's mood rises and his brush follows. Ts'ai Yung's recommendation on meditation and contemplation as a route to the highest achievement in art is among the earliest known writings in Chinese history. It is apparent that this idea must have developed from the influence of Taoist teachings.

Ts'ai Yung was the greatest calligrapher that China has ever produced. In his "Essential Record of Callig-

[29] Li Ssu's entire writings have been lost. This fragment of Li's work is quoted by Wei Su (eighth century) in Section I of his *Mu Sou*, or *Source Book of Calligraphy*.

raphy" Chang Yen-yuan of the Tang Period says that
Chinese calligraphy as an art was actually begun by
Ts'ai, who received his training from a religious master. Ts'ai taught the art to his daughter, Wen Chi, and
she in turn taught Chung Yuan, another renowned calligraphist. Chung Yuan taught Mme Wei, whose pupil
was the well-known Wang Hsi-chih. Several teacher-
pupil generations after Wang Hsi-chih came another
great Taoist calligraphist, Yu Shih-nan (seventh century), who expounded the Taoist philosophy on calligraphy. Since this is an important document I quote it
at length:

When one is going to hold the brush one must draw
back his vision and reverse his hearing, discard all thoughts
and concentrate on spiritual reality. When his mind is
tranquil and his breath harmonious his brush-work will
penetrate into subtlety. If his mind is not tranquil this
writing will not be straight. If his breath is not harmonious the character will fall short. . . . Tranquillity
means harmony in thoughtlessness.

Calligraphy contains the essence of art. The action of
moving the brush follows the principle of *wu wei* (nonassertion). Based upon the idea of *Yin* and *Yang* (nonaction
and action), the brush moves and stops. Grasping the essence of ten thousand things the characters are formed. To
understand nature and its changes is to know that the
constant is ever-moving. The art of calligraphy is mystical
and subtle. It bases itself upon the spiritual interfusion,
not upon artificial exertion. It requires the enlightenment
of one's mind but not sense perception. The form of the
characters is what you take in with your eyes, but eyes
have their limitations and obstructions. If one holds on to
only the outer structure of the characters one will be im-
peded by their material substance.

When one looks at water one detects the difference between the limitless and the limited. For instance, water
may be put in a round or square vase but the qualities of

roundness or squareness are by no means the properties of the water. The subtlety of the calligraphist's stroke, we may say, corresponds to the water and the roundness and the squareness of the water in the vase corresponds to the form of the characters. When one only holds on to the form of the character, even though what he sees appears to be one and the same, the limited and the limitless are indeed, different.

When there is evidence of a mood in the calligraphy it means that the mind was joyful. When the mind experiences joy it is no-mind, as it has interfused and identified with wonders. . . . In the transformation of his mind the calligrapher borrows the brush. It is not the brush that works the miracle. The transformation can only take place when the mind is tranquil and penetrates into the utmost subtlety. Thus spirit responds and mind is transparent. This is similar to plucking the harp; silken sounds and subtle melodies are produced at ease. In calligraphy inner serenity is released as the brush moves along. When the learner understands the meaning of *Tao*, his brush-work will follow the principle of *wu wei*, or nonassertion. However, if he should search for the beauty of mere appearances, he will remain ignorant.[30]

This is the philosophy of calligraphy but it can also be applied to painting. Chinese calligraphists (see Figures 8 and 9), just as other artists and poets, could not reach the highest level of production without the transformation of the mind. When expounding the basic principles of painting, George Rowley stresses also "the necessity of meditation and concentration in order to reach the highest state of creative readiness; then the artist could "grasp the natural without effort." [31] The principle of *wu wei* is entirely an action of creative intuition, which opens the wellsprings within man!

[30] Yü Shih-nan, *Pi Sui Lun*, or *Treatise on the Marrow of the Brush*, which appears in *Mu Sou*, Section 13.
[31] George Rowley, *op. cit.*, p. 35.

Fig. 8 *Pa-ta Shan-jen (Seventeenth Century) calligraphy (running script)*

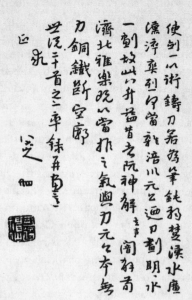

Fig. 9 *Wang Tsao-lin (Sixteenth Century) calligraphy (grass script)*

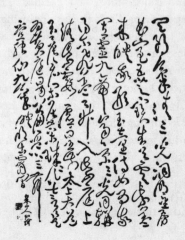

While the action of assertion, man's common tendency, is preconceptual and rational, it cannot penetrate the hidden recesses of creativity. The action of assertion is viewed from the externals of intellection, while the action of nonassertion is activated by the inner light. The former action is limited and finite, the latter free and limitless. The absolute freedom of the calligraphist's brush is the reflection of the inner serenity of the artist. Thus we have Yu Shih-nan's words that in calligraphy inner serenity is released, even as the brush moves along. It is the same feeling that the great master of painting, Ni Tsan, experienced when he said to his friends that the reason he painted bamboo was to release his inner serenity. Although Cheng Hao did not say so in so many words that he was releasing his inner joy when he wrote poems, one of which we have quoted in an earlier chapter, it is apparent from the very context of the lines that the poetry was a release of precisely the same nature.

The joy of releasing inner serenity is a by-product of creative intuition, which is identified with the ontological experience. Thus poetry, painting, and calligraphy, for their highest achievements, are all derived from a common ground. From a thorough study of one of these arts one can be led to a deep understanding of the others, because they all share primordial roots and radiate into the depths of one another. The inner relationship among these arts was observed by Ts'in Tsu-yung in his comments on the *Treatise of Painting* by Fang Hsun.

Poetry, literature, calligraphy and painting are closely related, often one enlightening the other. One may understand painting through the mastery of calligraphy; others may comprehend the essence of poetry through the mastery of painting; still others may understand painting through the mastery of poetry and literature. To lead the way to understanding we may enter by many doors.

As Whitehead puts it: "Art at its highest exemplifies the metaphysical doctrine of the interweaving of absoluteness upon relativity." And: "The final point is that the foundation of Reality, upon which Appearance rests, can never be neglected in the evaluation of Appearance." [32] Poetry, painting, and calligraphy each has its peculiar form of beauty, and yet to reach their common foundation in reality each of them follows the teaching of Taoism. In his introduction to his work, *Criticism of Calligraphy*, Chang Huai-huan, a great calligraphist of the eighth century, mentioned previously, gives us his inner experience, in words which may also be applied to poetry and painting:

Mind cannot consciously give to the hand and hand cannot consciously receive from the mind. Both mind and hand are one's own, but fail to grasp wonders when searching with intention. It is strange indeed! But when one's intuition identifies with Spiritual Reality and his brushstroke conveys the depth of the unconscious, he will be transformed and merge with the Divine, and his creation will be limitless. . . . His thoughtless thought penetrates the tip of his brush and his inner serenity permeates his whole being. When he pursues the spaceless and grasps the invisible it is as if the spiritual being were moving in and out. This is beyond what "words and images," "fishing nets" and "snares," could contain.[33]

[32] Whitehead, *Adventures in Ideas*, pp. 339-340.
[33] We may quote the expression from Chuang Tzu, Chapter 26, again: "The fishing net serves to catch the fish. Let us take the fish and forget about the net. The snare serves to catch the rabbit; let us take the rabbit and forget about the snare. Words serve to convey ideas; let us take the ideas and forget the words." This famous state-

The pursuit of the spaceless, grasp of the invisible, is to tap the depth of the unconscious and to transform one's self. This inner serenity will permeate his entire being and will be manifested in his brush work. The brush work serves only as a means to reveal the artist's inner state of being, which is the product of a transformation from the ego-form self to the nonego-form self. If the brush work is not rooted in the ground of the nonego-form self, Chinese critics would feel that the real meaning of art is missing. In the eleventh century Mi Yu-jen, the son of the great painter Mi Fei, who was also, incidentally, a great scholar and statesman, gave us his reasons for painting:

People in the world know that I am good at painting and they all want to have an example of my work. However, few of them understand why I paint. And unless they have the "wisdom of the eye" they can never know. My painting cannot be judged as those of the ancients and of the modern specialists. When we reach maturity in painting we are not attached to the mundane world whose affairs are nothing more than a single hair in the ocean. Whenever in the quiet of my room with my legs crossed I sit silently then I feel that I float up and down with the blue sky, vast and silent.

Floating in the vast and silent sky symbolically expresses the interfusion of the self with the universe. In Taoist words, it is being one with the ten thousand things. The ontological experience, as Mi Ju-jen says, is indispensable to the highest achievement in painting.

---

ment influenced Chinese Buddhist philosophy. As mentioned before, Tao Sheng (fourth century) revolutionized Chinese Buddhism by his application of this concept.

Concluding remarks

When the artist has achieved the ontological experience, his creative activities come into full bloom: into
their perfect fruition. But it is not the artist alone who
may look to the ontological experience as a source of
strength. Great leaders in human affairs—the statesman, the educator, the scientist—may, and in many
cases have, gone to the primordial source as their fountain of inspiration. Taoism is often said to posit a negative attitude toward the world, to encourage with-
drawal from life rather than active and joyous partici-
pation in it, and of course it is quite true that Lao Tzu
himself recommended the way of "losing and losing" to
reach to *Tao*. This is not rejection, however, but self-
realization. When man leaves his burden of anxiety
and fear behind him he attains an inner serenity and
reaches a higher and more integrated level of consciousness.

But this moving to a higher level does not mean giving up the world and its activities as being beneath us.

When Lao Tzu says, "To obtain *Tao* means to lose every day," he parallels this with another line, "To attain knowledge means to increase every day" (Ch. III). Life and its daily activities are not left behind but raised to a new height through perfect realization. To lose the burdens of fear and anxiety is not nihilistically to reject reality, but merely to cast aside the negative side of life—it is a fulfillment of the positive in dealing with the affairs of the world. Here again I quote Lao Tzu's own words:

As for where one stays, one values the proper place.
For the mind, one values its profundity.
For the friend, one values his kindness.
For words, one values sincerity.
For government, one values good order.
For affairs, one values ability.
For action, one values timeliness.

It is through these qualities that one's inner serenity is manifested. Thus in dealing with the affairs of the world one has inner serenity; in self-cultivation one never deviates from the necessities of practical life.

In concluding my book, I would like to recall the explanation under the final hexagram in the *Book of Changes*—the symbol of the not-yet-complete:

While the preceding hexagram offers an analogy to autumn, which forms the transition from summer to winter, this hexagram presents a parallel to spring, which leads out of winter's stagnation into the fruitful time of summer. With this helpful outlook the *Book of Changes* comes to its close.[1]

Now we have—so to speak—come to our last hexa-

[1] *I Ching*, the *Book of Changes*, Richard Wilhelm translation rendered into English by Cary P. Baynes, Vol. I, p. 265.

gram. It is not-yet-complete. But if we have glimpsed the meaning of *Tao* we have come to a new beginning, the path through the gardens of spring into the fruitful days of summer.